AF488219

Chasing the Red Dot

PEREGRINATIONS THROUGH 2024

Irene Genelin

Copyright © 2026 Authored and Published by Irene Genelin
All rights reserved. Updated May 29, 2026.

Book Cover created by Ani Cotter and Irene Genelin
Interior photography by Irene Genelin and Andy Cotter
Guest writing by Andy Cotter

Paperback ISBN: 979-8-9945090-0-5
EPUB ISBN: 979-8-9945090-1-2

I want to encourage the sharing of my work. Please feel free to quote my writing or share any part of this book if it resonates with you. If you'd like to purchase bulk copies of this book for gifting, please email me at igenelin@gmail.com

For Andy, Ani, and you—for picking up this book to learn more about my family's adventures and what I've learned.

Contents

Preface

As we prepared to sell our organic farm in Minnesota and begin our worldschooling adventure in 2019, my friend Tracy visited us. She brought my daughter, Ani, a pink blanket as a memento for our journey. I shared with Tracy how much I longed to stay connected with others online, yet felt self-conscious about posting our travels on social media. She suggested that instead of focusing on the trip itself, I share what I was learning along the way.

Slowly, I found my voice and began writing about our life. When I post, it feels as though I am bringing along those who can't travel right now, allowing them to experience a piece of the journey with us. Tracy is no longer alive, but I think of her often when I write; I am deeply grateful for her friendship and her encouragement to share my life.

Our first big trip after leaving the farm was a drive from Minnesota to St. Pierre and Miquelon, a French territory off the coast of Newfoundland. Some days we drove for up to ten hours. At the time, we didn't allow Ani, then four, to use any screens in the car. As we neared our destination, we took turns entertaining her in the backseat, all of us glancing longingly at the red dot on Google Maps. Andy said, "If we ever write a book, we should call it Chasing the Red Dot."

For years, I struggled with imposter syndrome, feeling unworthy of this travel life. I eventually brought these feelings to a Buddhist monk during a session at a temple in Portland, Oregon. I told her I felt guilty for living this life while so many others cannot. She suggested two things: first, to practice deep gratitude for what I have, and second, to make the most of it. One of my goals in writing is to share these experiences with you, which helps me honor the life I've been given.

My husband, Andy, makes traveling easier because he genuinely loves the logistics of planning and studying transportation schedules. One of the things that initially drew me to him was his international thinking. We met through a shared love of unicycling and have traveled the world together for competitions, long-distance tours, and now worldschooling with Ani.

Ani has brought countless experiences into my life, helping me clarify what I value. I want her to grow up living a healthy, grounded life—one filled with joy and a love of learning. I started and stopped writing this book several times over the past year, and she was the one who encouraged me to finish it. We are fortunate to learn alongside her as she pursues self-directed education. This book is an example of that philosophy in action; it is my first self-published work, and Ani even helped me design the cover.

Many families who choose to home-educate face resistance from extended family. I am deeply grateful to my parents, Mike and Kay, and to Andy's parents, Al and Joan, for supporting our choices—especially regarding Ani's education. I am also thankful to my friend Jodi, who shared her writing practice with me. What once felt intimidating now feels meditative, and I have come to enjoy documenting our experiences for others.

I love meeting people as we travel and sharing small, everyday moments—glimpses of different cultures, foods, and ways of living. I am so thankful to those of you who, over the years, encouraged me to write. This book is a collection of posts I shared in 2024, along with photographs taken by Andy or me.

At the beginning of this journey, Ani was nine years old. We were celebrating Christmas in Arizona and preparing for a trip to Vietnam to participate in the first "Traveling Village" alongside eighteen other families. This book follows our family through 2024 as we travel through Vietnam, Thailand, Japan, the United States, Italy, and Egypt.
Thank you for taking the time to purchase and read this book.

TUCSON, ARIZONA, USA

January 1st
This heart cactus photo was taken at the Desert Museum of
Tucson. Can you see all three of my family members? The pictures
of us are from Tucson, AZ, Ashland, OR, and Fort Collins, CO.
Editing this photo with Ani was a great way to spend the last part
of 2023

January 2nd

We have been making the most of our time in Tucson, Arizona, by visiting a few top sights: The Desert Museum, the Flandreau Science Center and Planetarium, and Sabino Canyon. We also met a family interested in learning how to unicycle when walking through Winterhaven. We stopped at the Schwinn display with a lit-up unicycle on it, and Brenda Noon Schmidt asked us for tips on learning to ride, as she had always wanted to learn to unicycle. We exchanged phone numbers and had several practice sessions with their family over the past two days. I always enjoy sharing the love of unicycling with others. I reflected that next year I will try to be even more of a unicycle ambassador by teaching others and doing things I love on a unicycle. Lately, it's been riding the curbs (skinnies) around Tucson. I love focusing 100% on the curb in front of me.

January 4th

Ani helped me go through our spices and prepare our mini spice kit to take with us on our travels to Southeast Asia. She practiced her handwriting while we smelled the different aromas. I still have a few spices from Romania (cloves and nutmeg). Living minimally means not having many things from our travels, but I always smile when using spices from a foreign country while cooking.

January 5th

We are embarking on our trip to Southeast Asia, flying to Vietnam on Saturday. We have been preparing for this trip for the past year. There were about 3 weeks recently, in November/December, when we weren't sure if we would be able to go, as Andy had a health scare. Andy had his annual health checkup last July, and his prostate-specific antigen (PSA) levels were a bit high. He then had his blood retaken to be sure it wasn't a false reading. Then, he had an MRI in Texas. Something was found that looked suspicious. Thanks to a good family friend, we could quickly connect with a urologist in Arizona, and he did a biopsy on Andy. Then we waited a week and found out that he had atypical cells in his prostate, but not cancer at this time.

January 5th
It is my father, Mike Genelin's, 76th Birthday today.

We filled our Airbnb with balloons last night after he was asleep, so he was surprised to find them this morning. We also celebrated with a piñata from the Piñata Factory, which we filled with items he loves (including a bag of Birchwood Blend Peace Coffee).

The piñata was a big hit with the whole family.

HANOI, VIETNAM

January 9th

After many hours and three different airplanes, we arrived in Hanoi, Vietnam. Our longest flight was from LAX to Taipei, Taiwan, which took just over 13 hours.

Observations so far:
*China Airlines had delicious airplane food. We ordered vegetarian meals as they are often tastier. I was delighted as I ate mushrooms and vegetables such as kabocha squash, lotus root, adzuki beans, tofu with celery, and other unique items.
*The airport in Taipei, Taiwan, has beautifully decorated waiting areas. Several of them highlight natural areas you can visit in Taiwan, and another focuses on green energy. Our boarding gate was decked out in butterflies.
*We started walking around Hanoi, Vietnam. The sense of space between people here is very slim. As you start walking across the street, motorbikes continue on their turning trajectory. If you stop walking, they will hit you; if you keep going, you pass by without incident. The sidewalks are narrow, as people sit on them to eat and to park motorbikes and vehicles.
*Ani and I rode our unicycles around today to get some groceries, and about half the people noticed us as we passed by and gave us some positive regard.
*I need to get comfortable again with my limited language knowledge. I go to the market for fresh food and hope the salesperson is kind and trustworthy, since I often don't understand the total cost of what I'm asking for. I will show them some bills in my hand, and they will take what is required and give me the change back. Sometimes, going to a small grocery store is more straightforward because prices are clearly labeled, and I can use my credit card to complete purchases. However, the allure of the fresh markets lies in the high quality of the products and the challenge of interacting with locals.
*The exchange rate is about 25,000 Vietnamese Dong to $1 United States dollar, so $50,000 is $2 USD.

January 10th

We are starting to meet other families in the Traveling Village. Having playmates for Ani, Andy, and me feels so good.

We are staying in a unique apartment that we found via Airbnb. The toilet is in our apartment's landing, between two bedrooms. So, when we need to use the bathroom or shower, we close the door and pull the curtain. Staying here made me reflect on a few things I've learned during our travels.

*There is no washing machine for clothes. No problem, I showered with my traveling undergarments and t-shirt and hung them up to dry. The humidity is so high that they aren't drying on their own. That's no problem. Put a fan on them to help them dry. I learned hand-washing on the unicycle tours we've been on and during our time in Ecuador.

*Putting toilet paper in the toilets here isn't recommended, as the septic systems are fragile. It is akin to our visit to several South American countries. Here, they also will often use a sprayer to wash the vagina after urinating. This reminds me of the practice of using a bidet, which is common in France and many other countries.

*I expect to see cockroaches, common in large buildings, especially in tropical climates. So far, I haven't, but it freaked me out the first time I did (in Vietnam in 2008). After living with them in Colombia in 2020 and singing La Cucaracha, I'm less afraid. Ani even held one when we visited the Bell Museum in Minnesota last summer. She said it tickled as the cockroach nibbled at the dead skin cells on her hand. I've even had two cockroaches star in a bedtime story; we named them Milk and Cookie, and they had a whole group of nymphs, each named after a different cookie (many from the Girl Scout cookie line). The story takes place in Getsemani, Colombia, in the town square, where we frequently visited while living there. We noticed many cockroaches living in the cracks of the sidewalk bricks. So, instead of being creeped out by these pests, the story made us remember a good time from our travels.

*We expect to cohabitate with insects as the weather is warm here. I haven't seen tiny ants in our small kitchen yet, but I'm prepared for them and know how to keep it clean, having lived in Hawaii. The Big Island of Hawaii had many ants that knew exactly where to look for food scraps.

*The sheets and pillowcases are floral-scented, as strong odors in laundry detergent are common. This is true everywhere we've lived, and we have learned to adapt by bringing our pillowcases. We put them over the pillow covers, which helps mask the odor. We also try to wash our clothes for this exact reason. The intensely perfumed laundry detergent often gives me a headache or makes Andy's nose run.

Ani chatting with a friend inTaipei

BB on the plane

Getting much needed pho soup in Hanoi

HANOI + NINH BINH, VIETNAM

January 12th

In Hanoi, we went to a hot pot restaurant called Fridays for lunch with a few other families. I had no idea how to cook with this heating device. After putting too much oil on the table's heating tray and having bits splatter onto the children, the waiter kindly came to our rescue and showed us how to cook the raw meat and veggies on our table properly. We also discovered there were paper bibs we could wear to protect our clothes. We had a big bowl of soup to cook the meat and veggies in. After the waiter demonstrated how to assemble the spring roll correctly, we finally felt more at ease. It was a humbling experience!

On our last night in Hanoi, I heard a rustling sound behind the sink and some chattering, the sound of a rat. While keeping my calm (Ani and I were in one room, and I didn't want to freak her out), I got out of bed, opened our door to the hallway, and started pulling everything out from underneath the sink to see if I could scare whatever it was out of our apartment. I didn't see anything, but I tried to scare it away from that area by pulling the drawers and banging on the built-in shelves. I discovered quite a bit of mold under the kitchen sink. At first, I left the doors open to air it out, then realized that was a terrible idea, as we smelled more mold in the bedroom while trying to sleep. I closed the doors and imagined a protective bubble around us while we drifted off to sleep. I learned that trick from someone in Costa Rica who was camping in a place teeming with tropical creatures, including scorpions. She said she imagined herself wrapped in a protective bubble while sleeping, so no creatures would bother her. It worked for her and us as we got through the night, but I am glad to no longer be at that Airbnb.

We took a train to Ninh Binh and had a few hours between checking out of the Airbnb and our train's departure. The families met and hung out at the train station, waiting for the train to leave at 3:30 pm. I wasn't feeling great.

My body had chills, and I wasn't hungry at all. I think it was a combo of jet lag/new foods/mold/crappy sleep that got me. Thankfully, on the train, I could take the top bunk and sleep a little while my body recovered. Being with the other families helped pass the time, and it was fun to exchange stories and play games with the kids along the way. Outside the train window, I saw water buffaloes and many fields full of rice paddies. I am relieved to be away from the busy city of Hanoi, where there is less pollution from motorbikes and vehicles.

I slept well last night, and today, I feel much better. Ani has a sore throat, so we stayed home at our new hotel (which is really clean, thank goodness!). Andy is on a tour with the rest of the families. He is taking pictures to share with us when he returns.

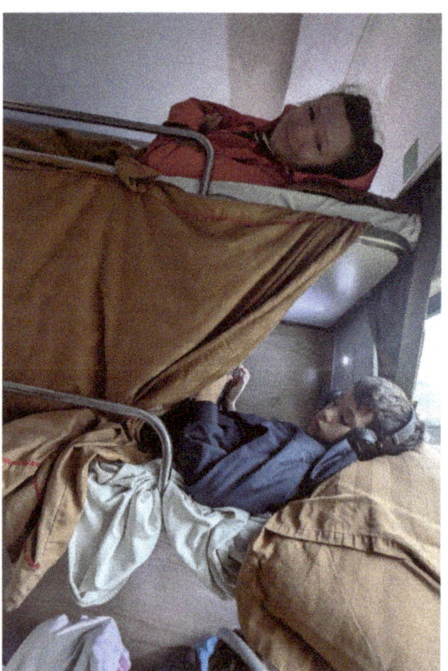

Irene and Noah on the train

Hot Pot at Fridays Restaurant

NINH BINH, VIETNAM

January 13th

I'm reading a book called "Lost Connections" by Johann Hari. Johann makes a compelling case that the current mental health crisis is driven by the disconnection that has become rife in modern life and proposes various types of reconnection as antidotes.

I just read a passage in the book where Johann talks about his friend Rachel. After years of envying what others had or were experiencing, Rachel discovered an ancient technique called "sympathetic joy." It is a method for cultivating "the opposite of jealousy or envy... It's simply feeling happy for other people."

"You close your eyes and picture yourself. You imagine something good happening to you – falling in love or writing something you're proud of. You feel the joy that would come from that. You let it flow through you. Then you picture somebody you love and imagine something wonderful happening for them. You feel the joy from that, and you let that, too, flow through you."

You meditate this way every day for 15 minutes, continuing to think of others and to imagine something wonderful happening for them. Eventually, you start to feel that their joy is something that you can share with them.

I pondered this as I encouraged Andy to join a group tour in Ninh Binh yesterday, while I stayed home with a sick Ani. Instead of feeling left out or jealous, I was happy he could go spend time exploring and connecting with the other families in our traveling village. Especially considering his recent health scare, I'm so glad he is here with us and able to see and do things.

Today, Ani is a little better, so we could head into town for lunch and take in the beautiful rice paddies and the fascinating flora and fauna of Ninh Binh.

This practice of sympathetic joy reminds me of the loving-kindness meditation that Sharon Salzburg has helped popularize in the West. Have you ever meditated in this way?

Here are pictures from Andy's tour in Ninh Binh. In the bottom photo, he is wearing a red rain jacket.

NINH BINH + HOI AN, VIETNAM

January 15th

We arrived in Hoi An this morning after taking the night train from
Ninh Binh. Our villa host, Cherry, is fantastic. The villa is clean,
recently remodeled, and free of mold. This evening, she organized
one of the two group meals for us. We ate well (spring rolls, fried
rice, banana flower salad, pancakes wrapped with greens and
dipped in peanut sauce, fried rice paper with tomato chutney,
roasted eggplant, and, for the meat eaters, pho). It was amazing.
While she welcomed us to her villa and arranged a meal for
tonight, she is also helping another group from our Traveling
Village find a new place to stay after they discovered mold in their
accommodation that was too much to live with. Cherry said it was
common during the pandemic for hotel owners to neglect proper
ventilation, leading to the mold problem. That group is staying in a
hotel tonight and hopes to find a new place for the next 5 weeks
by tomorrow night.

Ani had a fever yesterday, so we stayed in our hotel room all day
to let her rest. After waking up and eating a few bites, she fell back
asleep until 3:30 pm. Thankfully, overnight on the train, her fever
subsided, and she is feeling better today, although still not back to
her usual self. I am thankful for Barbara, who shared some cold
medicine with us to give to Ani, as she needed something. I used
Google Translate to translate the medicine fact sheet from
Vietnamese to English to understand what I was giving her and
find the correct dosage. It helped her fall asleep without coughing.

Yesterday, I bicycled to Mua Caves, one of the places Andy and
the group had seen a few days earlier. At the same time, Ani
rested, and Andy stayed with her. The bicycle I rode was rickety
but stayed together almost the entire journey. I got a flat front tire
and had to walk the last mile home.
On my handlebars were two bags of pho noodle soup. Yes, bags,
as the small mom-and-pop shop I stopped at outside the main
drag didn't have proper to-go containers.

Irene and a pug nosed dog in Ninh Binh

The woman who worked there asked me, via Google Translate, whether I had a bowl at my hotel or needed to borrow one from her. I reassured her that I could source something. In the end, I couldn't find one, so I drained the broth into a cup, and we ate the noodles from the plastic bag. I think pho is not a to-go food; it is best enjoyed fresh at a restaurant.

Cemetery marker

Irene and Ani in Hoi An

Holiday Villa, our home in Hoi An for five weeks

Andy and Ani looking from our room out to the pool

One of the delicious dishes served to us on our first night at the Holiday Villa

HOI AN, VIETNAM

January 17th

We are starting to settle into our Villa in Hoi An. One of the adults, Martin, loves playing with kids, so it is common to see him playing charades and joking with them. It is delightful to have other trusted adults around us. We are also experimenting with leaving Ani alone at the villa for an hour or so while Andy and I go for a walk. It is great to know that, should she need something, there are many other adults around to help her. She can also contact us via FB Messenger.

Yesterday, I consulted with the dentist about why my tooth was aching. They could take an X-ray (cost $4 USD) and found no infection. The dentist adjusted my night guard to prevent my teeth from clashing when I grind at night. It made a huge difference, and I already feel better after one night's sleep. Going to a medical place in a different country is always scary, as you never know what to expect. Again, I was surprised at the low cost and ease of working with a dentist in another country.

We met up with almost all the other traveling families at the beach today. Andy and Ani rode bicycles there, and I rode my 20" unicycle the 3 miles to the beach. I got so many positive comments and thumbs up. One motorbike rider followed me and filmed me, so I took out my phone and took a film of him filming me. He smiled, and we had a laugh after he passed me.

I'm still not used to the smell of gas while walking the busier streets in town. It is from motorbikes. I'll walk during quieter times so I don't have to smell it as much. Yesterday, when I rode my unicycle home, I went past a school where the adults were all outside on their motorbikes, waiting to pick up their children. I carefully zigzagged through the motorbikes and waved to the children, who were surprised to see me riding on one wheel.

Ani and Andy on bike

BB and Octopus

Rice paddies at sunset

January 18

Today, we had our first group fitness training with Andrea as our leader. We did a variety of lunges, squats, sit-ups, push-ups, and shuttle runs. My upper body is very sore, especially after working out with Andrea yesterday morning. My goal is to strengthen my arms while we are here, and I'm grateful for the guidance and the group to train with!

This evening, I went on a vegan street food tour. It ended up being just me and the guide, Nguyên. She has an American name, Annie, by which she introduced herself. Later, she shared her Vietnamese name with me. We started with a vegan Bahn Mi. I learned that when the French occupied Vietnam, they introduced the baguette to this culture. Instead of importing wheat flour from abroad, the Vietnamese have learned to make bread from rice flour or a mix of wheat and rice. We sampled various dishes and ended the tour with a subtly sweet black sesame sweet potato soup.

Irene in Old Town crossing a bridge

Irene and a Bahn Mi

Ani creating tooth powder

January 19th

Today, a portion of our group visited the Hoi An Eco-Hub. It houses the Green Youth Collective and Refillables Hoi An. They had a variety of stations set up for us. Some of my favorites were making tooth powder, creating a reusable grocery bag from a t-shirt, creating yarn from a shirt, holding the black soldier fly larvae, and painting seed packages to give away flower seeds. There were a few more stations I didn't have a chance to visit.

Ani loved the attention she received from one of the cats at the Eco-Hub.

We went for dinner and a playdate with some other families at Dingos Deli, which served food and had a nice sandy playground for the young children to play in. I enjoyed getting to know the other families and reflected on how much more independent Ani is at age 9. She happily played in the sand, alone and with the other kids. In contrast, the other parents took turns interacting with their younger children. Each phase of life offers its joys and challenges. Tonight, I am grateful for the independence that comes with age nine and for sleeping through the night.

January 20th

Today, we had the welcome party for the Traveling Village at the Roving Chill House. It is a beautiful space next to rice paddies. The workgroup that put this together did a fantastic job. There was an activity book for the children, a photo of all the families, a fan, a leather keychain with each child's name, and a few candies for each child. The activity book encouraged each child to write the name of each family member and their country beside the family's photo.

The meal consisted of small bites of spring rolls, banh mi sandwiches, rice, steamed vegetables, and fresh fruit juice. Our group has a variety of food sensitivities (vegetarians, vegans, grain-free, egg-free, and dairy-free), yet we managed to find food that suited everyone. I was impressed!

An artist named Minh was painting a scene that represented the village. He was going to make a copy of the final piece for each family to take home as a memento from Vietnam. Ani really wanted to help him paint, so Andy asked if she could also paint, and he gave her some paint and a piece of paper to work on. This inspired a few other children, who took their paint palettes and paper over to a view overlooking the rice paddies.

Ani and I stayed for about two hours, and then we came back to our Villa. I am excited to be with many other families, but I thrive in smaller groups. Two hours was great for me, and then Ani and I had some quiet time listening to an audiobook and doing art together. We will have communal meals twice a week with the entire group (about 80 people). As we get to know more people, we will find it easier to stay longer at the gatherings.

I used our small kitchen for the first time today, cooking eggs and noodles for Ani and reheating some leftovers for myself. I also made golden milk with soy milk and spices. It feels good to cook again and find some daily normalcy. The food selection in Vietnam is amazing, yet it is nice to make some simple dishes.

Erin and Ani with their welcome gear

Ani at the Roving Chill House

Irene's unicycle near flowers that are grown for the Tết Holiday

January 22nd

Moments from the past few days:

*Participating in a disco birthday party with the other Traveling Village families. Realizing that all the adults there also have kids and know how to make them feel comfortable and loved. Feeling relieved, I realize I am not the only one worried about their child at a large gathering.

*I participated in a basketball game with four other men. We played three games, and they let me try the first game on my unicycle. I haven't played basketball on foot since middle school (I prefer playing unicycle basketball), but it was fun.

*Seeing people light up when I ride my unicycle past them. Today, I had one motor scooter person follow me for a while, then come right up beside me and open his palm so I could give him a low five. I also had a mother and her son follow me on a motor scooter, with the little boy laughing delightedly at the absurdity of seeing a woman on a unicycle. I went to a tailor shop to pick up a dress, and all the employees (about 15) came out to the curb to watch me get on and ride away. I waved at them as I left.

*I spent this morning Painting with @minh.artist in his home studio. He gave Ani and me a low-key painting lesson, and I left feeling very calm and relaxed. We hope to go again for another painting session.

*Petting many cats at Jack's Cat Cafe. They care for over 100 cats (all available for adoption). Their mission is to slow/stop the cat meat industry in Vietnam and save as many cats as they can. I have many emotions after visiting this place. I was raised to believe cats are pets, and I don't like the idea of eating them, but I realize we are in a completely different culture. Is it right to come into a new country and try to change things?

*At lunch today, I used an app that asks open-ended questions to stir up our normal family conversation as we waited for our food to arrive. When I asked, "How can we have more fun?" Ani said, in a calm tone, "We're having the time of our lives!" We are so lucky." I was floored by her response, and I agree—we are fortunate to be living this life right now.

Ani at Jack's Cat Cafe

Painting with Minh

Irene and Ani painting

January 26th

This week, the weather has been rainy here. It has been so rainy that, at times, the street near our villa struggles to drain. I wore flip-flops and walked through ankle-deep rain when I needed to get out, and the puddles drained after the rain stopped. Today, we finally have some sunshine, and it feels wonderful.

Ani caught a stomach bug a few days ago that was spreading among the children. She stopped vomiting yesterday morning and has been recovering since. She has low energy, but she is getting better.

We continue to taste amazing Vietnamese foods. The food features rice, meat, tofu, vegetables, and herbs to support digestion and flavor. There is always a sauce of some kind – fish sauce, soy sauce, and little red chilis that float in the sauce or are served with the dish. I am enjoying their heat; it is not overwhelmingly hot, but rather medium, adding flavor to the dish. Yesterday, I participated in a cooking class with several other families. We visited the Ba Le local market, where fresh tofu was made and cut into blocks. Our guide showed us where rice is husked and milled. We saw a stand full of garlic that sold out every day. We made a variety of traditional Vietnamese dishes in the cooking class.

I realized that the horns people use in traffic here are a courtesy, letting you know you are about to be passed or that a vehicle is coming around a blind corner. Once I realized I wasn't being honked at for doing something wrong, my experience of hearing the horns changed, and I felt I could ride in traffic safely. It feels safer to unicycle on the street than to walk, as the sidewalks are used for parking motorbikes, selling flowers, and burning small fires with offerings to ancestors. The sidewalks are also uneven, so you have to watch where you step.

Last Wednesday, we attended another low-key art session with Minh. Another family joined us, and seeing how we all found our way to creativity at Minh and Vivian's home was enjoyable.

Last Tuesday evening, we had a communal meal that was absolutely beautiful. There were live cooking stations with chefs creating stir-fried noodles, Vietnamese pancakes, and other items based on your choice. It was pouring that evening, so we were all together under a covered area. The only downside to this was that my nose was irritated by the smoke at the cooking stations. There are many scents here that I am getting used to. There are often incense offerings in the sidewalk cracks. The ceremonial offerings to ancestors are curious to see – they burn fake money and even fake phones (made from paper) so their ancestors can have them in the afterlife. Cherry (our villa host) said that sometimes tourists mistake them for toys and will bring these paper phones home. This makes the Vietnamese laugh.

Painting Minh with friends

Popular garlic stand

Irene at the cooking class

UNO and spring roll

January 30th

One of my goals this year is to be a unicycle ambassador, sharing my love of unicycling with the world. So far, we have started teaching Minh and another friend from the Traveling Village how to ride. There is more interest, so we can teach several more by the time this trip is through. I used to be very competitive in unicycling, and I miss the intensity and focus of that period of my life. I recognize now that in family life, the intensity shifts and changes from focusing on yourself and training to ensuring your child survives and thrives. I am nurturing a new focus in unicycling, connecting with others, making them smile by riding on the streets, and teaching them how to ride. How have you kept your passions alive from before kids?

Teaching Minh to unicycle

Irene's unicycle near flowers that are grown for the Tết Holiday

Bánh chưng cake

Orchid flowers

Andy and Ani unicycling in Old Town

January 31st

Moments from the past few days:

*Last weekend, I caught the virus that's going around, and while I didn't throw up, my body emptied itself, and I wasn't hungry at all. I didn't eat at all on Saturday, and slept most of the day. Thankfully, I had a clean, comfortable bed to sleep in, and the worst of it lasted only a few days.

*Teaching Minh to unicycle was as enjoyable as visiting Viviana and Minh after the lesson at their home. They shared a local Tết (Vietnamese New Year) treat: Bánh chưng, a dish of rice, beans, and pork. Viviana shared Uyen Ninh's Instagram page with me (@Uyenninh), a Vietnamese woman living with her German boyfriend in Germany. She makes funny videos about the cultural differences between the two countries. They make me laugh. If you're looking for a good laugh, check her out.

*Ani has been missing familiar foods. It was so much so that Ani and I left the communal meal yesterday to come back and boil some tri-colored pasta for Ani for lunch.

I brought some vegan food to the Villa, and we enjoyed spending time together eating and playing cards. I visited a grocery store called Moon Milk, which carries a variety of Western foods, and smiled when I found Old El Paso Refried Beans. In the US, we always search out organic refried beans (we like Trader Joe's), but abroad, I love finding this brand. It brings comfort and a taste of home. When we lived in Colombia, I bought up several bags of their beans during our two-month stay. Moon Milk also has delicious quality bread. We ate sourdough bread for lunch today with avocado and eggs.

*We're figuring out a rhythm for organizing ourselves as a village. We're using Google Calendar, WhatsApp, and Slack to communicate. There always seems to be something we can join or someone to talk to. I've found quiet afternoons in our room a good way to recharge.

Ani carving wood

A laughing Buddha and Irene

Andy, Irene, and Ani with dancing dragons

February 4th

The Traveling Village offers many activities. Sometimes we must remind ourselves that we don't have to do everything, although the fear of missing out is real. For our family, having downtime in our room to do art, listen to audiobooks, or just chill by ourselves is rejuvenating. Nearly every day, there is some kind of community-oriented exercise - working out with Andrea, doing body weight workouts, playing soccer, swimming at the beach, or playing basketball. I am enjoying unicycling around town, getting from one place to another. The other day, I rode 11 miles on my 20" unicycle, which is a far distance for such a small wheel.

Last night, we had a communal meal at The Field restaurant, which is near rice paddies and has a big open space for the children to run and play. Parents entertained the young children while the tweens and teens played on their own, splitting into boys' and girls' groups. At one point, there were at least six dads with toddlers in their arms, pretending to zoom around as airplanes on the lawn. It was sweet to see the children grow comfortable with other adults and to watch the entertainment with the young children.

Irene and Ani Urban sketching

Last week, we participated in one of the first Urban Sketch Meet-Ups for the local Hoi An Chapter. Minh and his wife, Viviana, are trying to start an official group here. They must have a certain number of meet-ups before the national organization recognizes them. Several members of the Traveling Village met to sketch at the Bà Mụ Temple. I appreciated being in the presence of others while engaging in a quiet, focused activity rather than a loud one.

February 5th

Yesterday I woke up feeling tired. I had organized an excursion to Da Nang for later in the day, complete with a stop to search for one of the few Geocaches in Vietnam, and a visit to the Dragon Bridge to see it blow fire and water at 9 pm. Then I quickly realized that the excursion didn't sound fun; I needed a day of rest. We visited the lantern-making workshop and spoke with a few other families who had expressed interest. They also understood our need for quiet. Some also took the day off; others went on their own, and we heard about their experiences at breakfast this morning.

I gave Andy a haircut. We went to Miss H.A.'s coffee shop, which overlooks rice paddies, and saw the sunset. There, I heard a strange song with the lyrics, "I admit I'm lactose intolerant." That made me laugh and then repeat it, as I am lactose intolerant, but this was the first time I heard someone sing it in a song.

I bicycled into the old town and found a second-hand shop. I started looking through the dresses, then jumped back and yelled when I saw a gecko at the neck of one. The shop attendant found the gecko (his tail hanging out of the collar) and rehomed him outside. I was able to calm down and keep browsing, happily. I thank all those years on the farm for making me comfortable with mice, frogs, gophers, and more. This gecko didn't harm me, although he gave me a good scare. I found six pieces of clothes for $18 USD! This makes me happy. I spent at least an hour browsing Pinterest for dresses and linen clothes I might like to have made for myself (there are so many tailor shops here in Hoi An), but really, finding second-hand clothes that fit me well and are reasonably priced is my preference.

Just down the street was the Precious Heritage Art Gallery and Museum. https://www.rehahnphotographer.com/
It is filled with beautiful photographs by French photographer Réhahn. He builds a connection with his subject before even taking out the camera. After seeing his work, I almost feel proud of the wrinkles that are starting to show on my face.

The way he captures his older subjects makes their beauty shine, whether they are wrinkly, have stained teeth or hands, or have no teeth left at all.
It is worth visiting if you are in Hoi An, or exploring his website if you are elsewhere.

Miss H.A.'s Coffee Shop

DA NANG, VIETNAM

February 7th

Today we went to Da Nang to see the marble statues at Marble Mountain, take a graffiti workshop, and eat delicious pizza from Pizza 4P's. At breakfast this morning, I mentioned our plan to our villa host, Cherry, and she arranged a private car for us so we wouldn't have to wait for Grab pickups (like Uber or Lyft car-share apps) at each destination. It was also less expensive. Another reason we feel lucky to have Cherry as our host!

The graffiti workshop was held at Not Pop, a store that sells spray paint and offers surfing lessons. Last year, they organized a large mural-painting festival called Nam Jam, where many artists gathered to paint murals on the walls around their business. They are planning another for this spring; it will be their second Nam Jam Festival.

I enjoyed learning to sketch our mural idea in chalk and to use a spray can and roller to fill in the design. At first, I wanted to paint the whole wall white, but the instructor told me to sketch the design over the paint already on the wall so we wouldn't use as much paint and it would dry faster. Some artists use a projector to get their design on the wall, while others use a doodle or a lazy grid system.

After the workshop, we went to Pizza 4Ps (Pizza for Peace) and ate one of the best pizzas of our lives. https://pizza4ps.com/ This company started after the owner was searching for happiness after his best friend died by suicide. After contemplating the question "What is happiness?" while experimenting with pizza, he realized people were always happier after a pizza party. So, he opened this business and sources ingredients from local farms. There are now multiple stores across several countries. I highly recommend a visit!

Graffiti Workshop

Pizza at Pizza 4 P's

February 9th

Tonight is the eve of Tết; we have been preparing for the past few days by buying groceries and watching the intensity of the traffic and preparations around us. At midnight tonight, it will be officially Tết, the Lunar New Year.

On Tết, we have learned it is bad form to take out the trash or sweep. It is common to give envelopes with lucky money to family members. We plan to visit a local pagoda in the morning.

Today, we had a communal lunch at Bếp Tre, a beautifully designed building. I really loved the flat roads and the curbs to unicycle on. Before our lunch was served, I practiced coasting and riding along some curbs.

Our artist friend, Minh, revealed the big painting he created of the Traveling Village today. It was cool to feel the crowd's excitement as he unveiled it. He had smaller prints for our families to take home, and Nikolaj purchased the large print to return to Denmark.

At times Ani has opened up and started playing with the children staying at our villa, and at other times she has craved quiet time, by listening to audiobooks and doing art. Today, at lunch, she realized that everyone in a new restaurant setting was too much for her, so she put on her headset, did some art, and swung on the swing by herself. We checked in with her a few times, but she was content, and I was happy she could regulate herself this way.

Minh about to reveal the large painting

Family photo at the temple

Irene unicycling

Ivana, Silja, and Ani at the communal meal

February 10th
Happy Lunar New Year!

This morning, we celebrated Tết by visiting a local pagoda with our Villa host, Cherry Phương Hiền. It was busy, with many people there to pray and light incense for their ancestors.

Andy and I rented traditional Vietnamese outfits for 24 hours, and I was surprised by how comfortable the dress and pants were. They were also very light and cool (not sweltering hot). Ani wore the new items she had made at the tailor's and is saving her traditional outfit to wear another time.
Typically, you wear new clothes to welcome yourself to the New Year.

Ivana held a cacao ceremony with breath work and yin yoga. The cacao was from Guatemala. It was my first cacao ceremony, and it was exciting.

We had a very low-key day. The streets were quiet, and most shops were closed.

Ani wearing her new clothes at the pagoda

Hien (Cherry), Minh (Sunlight), Irene, and Ani at the pagoda

February 14th

We have one week left in Vietnam. During the Lunar New Year holiday, many shops are closed. Those that are still open will often have many people around them.

I thought the holiday would slow things down, but instead, I find communal living and the traveling village just as busy. We need to carve out time to be alone and rejuvenate. Today, Ani and I stayed behind during an excursion several other families took to Ba Na Hills Amusement Park. Andy decided to go, and he is taking pictures to share with us when he returns. Ani and I are enjoying our day together. We recorded a Worldschooling Space Podcast and went for lunch at Nourish, where we did art together and ate delicious food. If you'd like to listen to the podcast, please visit: https://tinyurl.com/2ydz3rdc

Irene and Ani outside of Nourish after our lunch and art date

Andy and I continue to give unicycle lessons to village members. We've now taught six adults and four children the basics of getting on and starting to ride.

I signed up for a 23 km trail-running race on May 11th in Japan. Andy is also signed up. I asked Ani and some of our village friends about taking the day to have both Andy and me run this race, and because we are with the village, it is possible for us to do this together!

Today is Valentine's Day. I haven't given it much focus, as it is usually promoted for commercial purposes. But it does make me think of those I hold near and dear. May you, dear reader, have a good day today, celebrating Love - for the Earth, yourself, and your loved ones.

Minh painting Ani's face

Ani with face paint like a panda

February 18th

We participated in a three-day Bánh Chưng (Vietnamese Sticky Rice Cake) making session hosted by Minh and Viviana at their home.

Bánh Chưng has a long history in Vietnamese culinary culture and is a beloved dish during Tet. This cake expresses gratitude to the ancestors, the earth, and the sky, and underscores the central role of rice and nature in Vietnamese culture.

They can be made with pork in the center (typically square) or as a vegetarian option (generally cylindrical). They consist of glutinous rice soaked overnight in pandan-flavored water, mung beans soaked overnight, and pork marinated with shallots and spices, or with peanuts, at the center.

You assemble the Bánh Chưng using banana leaves cut to shape and frozen overnight, then tie them with a string and boil the cakes for 8-12 hours in water. Minh and Viviana made a campfire and even brought out a tent to sleep outside while our cakes cooked. It was a fun experience. Several of us returned on the third day (Saturday) to test the final result. We dipped the Bánh Chưng in soy sauce with chili paste and savored all of the effort. These Bánh Chưng will last for a while in the fridge. You can also cut and fry them to make the edges crispy (which we did for lunch today).

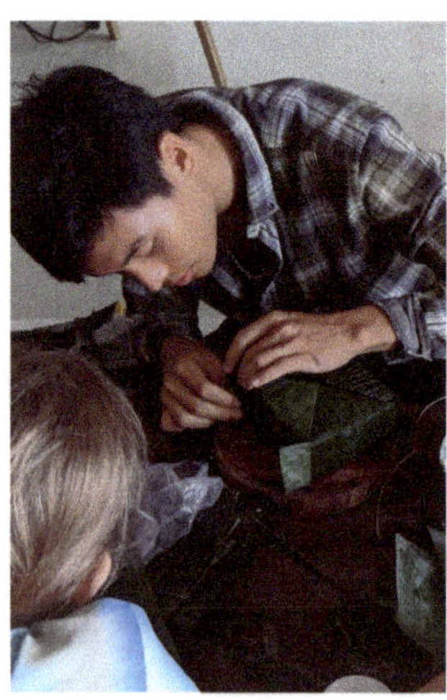

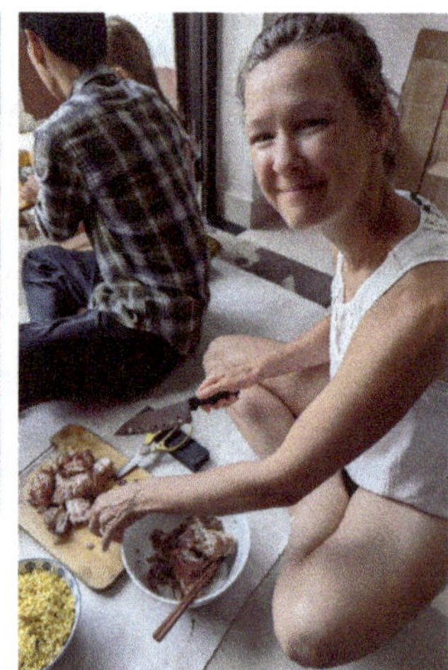

I participated in a croquette-making class Chef Nick hosted here at our Villa. This process took two days. On the first day, in the afternoon, he made a beef rendang stew using beef, lemon grass, garlic, onions, chili, salt, pepper, and coconut milk. We joined him in the evening, and he gave us a presentation about croquettes and showed us pictures of the croquettes he created for his restaurant in the Netherlands. Then we separated the liquid from the stew and shredded the beef. Next, he showed us how to make a roux using butter and flour, then mix in the liquid, some gelatin sheets, and finally, the shredded beef. This was put in the fridge overnight to chill.

The next night, we met again to shape the croquettes, roll them in flour, dip them in milk, then in breadcrumbs, and fry them. Chef Nick found several Vietnamese ciders to sample when the croquettes were hot. I sampled both, and they tasted amazing (even though I normally don't eat much dairy or drink alcohol). I think the atmosphere and quality of the final product helped me digest everything well.

We also played soccer and basketball (with three Vietnamese people and our village members, which made for a fun full-court game), and I went for a run. I'm also expanding my hair-cutting techniques by giving haircuts to several members of the village. I find this a fun challenge and a worthwhile artistic endeavor. I realize I enjoy small one-on-one meetings, which is what a haircut is.

Croquettes

Artwork by Ani

February 21st

Our last days in Vietnam

The last few days in a location are always bittersweet for me. I try to appreciate the things that have become commonplace – the beautiful breakfasts we received at our Villa, the friendly presence of Cherry's parents at the Villa (we took to calling them Grandma and Grandpa. Grandpa's name in Vietnamese if pronounced wrong sounds like the same word for 'poop', so I thought it was best to stick to Grandpa). Last night, Grandma helped me take down my clothes from the line at the back of the villa, and while I hadn't been able to communicate with her very much because of the language barrier, this simple act was very warm and kind. The colorful streets and Tet decorations, cycling in the stream of traffic now that I know the pattern, the lovely lady Bi at the Healing House, who has given me and several other Villagers massages and herbal tea gifts with each visit.

Yesterday, in the midst of packing, I asked myself why I felt sluggish and wanted to cry. I realized it is because I feel it goes against natural tendencies to create roots in one location. Just as we discovered where to buy groceries, found a good rhythm in our living environment, met some lovely locals, and recognized common strangers who help us in the markets and shops, we change our location. It is also exciting to open oneself to the unknown. I admit I was hesitant to even come to the Traveling Village a year ago when Andy really started digging in. The whole concept seemed overwhelming to me, and I couldn't fathom living in a community, yet, little by little, Andy and I talked about it, and we met more interested people online. Now that we've completed ⅓ of the trip, I am so glad that I came. The communal living in our Villa offered way more good than bad, and I feel like I know the others much better because of the informal conversations and chance encounters we had living so close.

Moments of joy from co-living were: getting to know K at breakfast by sharing his passion for art, kids disco parties that I would participate in, sharing impromptu dinners with Andrea and other kids, impromptu unicycle lessons, learning how to make croquettes from Nick, the countless times Andy and I were able to participate in one activity together because Ani had a community and felt safe to stay at the Villa on her own, seeing Ani go to town with E and D on their own for the first time, learning body weight exercises from Andrea, eating breakfast together everyday, sharing three delicious communal meals at the Villa, singing karaoke (even thought I wasn't convinced at first that it would be a good idea), and the birthday disco with so many other families that just wanted their kids to feel safe and loved while dancing.

Ani with her favorite breakfast bhan mi with scrambled eggs

Cherry, Irene, and Ani

Hoi An Holiday Villa at night

HOI AN, VIETNAM, AND LANGKAWI, MALAYSIA
February 21st
Happy Birthday to Andy!
He celebrated turning 55 with a farewell dinner at Hoi An Holiday Villa, and a cake upon our arrival in Malaysia at our Airbnb in Langkawi.

Malaysian BDay cake

Andy with a cake from Cherry

Rice paddies in Hoi An

Andy with his BDay gift from Ani

Ani with a bike heading to the beach

Minecraft figurines that Ani made as gifts

MALAYSIA

February 24th

Expectations and reality of living in tropical climates:
E, crouched over with her hand in the pond, letting small fish with rainbow colored fins eat dead skin cells from her palm. It feels like small kisses, slightly ticklish. My palm opens wide in the water, and some tadpoles rest while their fish friends nibble away.
Showering four times daily to smell fresh, remove sweat, and stay cool.

The heat is so high that the 'real feel' is 119 degrees Fahrenheit (48 Celsius).

There is a beautiful bird song, one specific to the island of Langkawi, Malaysia, outside our bedroom window. I hear it over the A/C set to 80 degrees, which is helping my body adjust to this extreme heat.

Staying back from outings with friends allows my body and Ani's body to rest and acclimate. I feel like I am missing out. Remembering that rest is also essential. Feeling like I am missing out, over and over again.

I am afraid to swim because of jellyfish.

I'm swimming, feeling relief. Sweet evaporation. I feel sticky and salty. I'm rinsing off in a foot bath because I don't have Malaysian Ringgit currency to pay for a shower (which costs $.20). I'm not fussing with an ATM for just one day.

Coconut water. Cools the body. This one is a young coconut. Yes! The waitress cracks it open, and I spoon out smooth jelly flesh, savor it in my mouth, then dig in again.

A huge noise in the bathroom in the early hours of the morning wakes me. Andy had a frog jump onto his foot while he was urinating in the toilet.

Mosquitos. Netting is like a gift from the gods.

I see a giant centipede in our tropical housing. It is moving so slowly. Surely it will stay there while I brush my teeth and wash my face. Then I will remove it. It is gone when I look again. I say nothing, not wanting to scare Ani.

Marveling at the beauty of the water, tropical plants, and flowers. Many flowers look similar, yet slightly different from those I've seen before.

I admired a beautiful monkey crossing the road. I walked closer and was frightened by another monkey. I believe he was scaring me away from his territory. I Googled how to handle monkeys in Thailand. Can I really make an O with my mouth, raise my eyebrows, and lean my chest and neck forward if faced with an aggressive one? I felt grateful for our tropical room, with a centipede and a frog to shelter me from the monkeys and the heat.

There are many cats in Thailand. Is there no cat meat trade here like there was in Vietnam?

Passion fruit. Sour, sweet, crunchy. The outside of the fruit is like a weathered face, crinkly and purple. You would certainly pass it up if you didn't know the Inside is a flavor explosion.

While walking, I see a lot of trash along the roads. When it is abundant, it feels pointless to pick any up. Would it make a difference? Is there recycling here? Where does an island put all of its trash?

KOH LANTA, THAILAND

March 1st

Thailand is making me a morning person. The slightly cooler temperature at 7 am is the best time to run, practice yoga, or do body strength exercises.

After searching for a human-powered mode of transportation for Andy and Ani (like a bicycle with a seat on the back), we found nothing, so we rented a motor scooter. We named it the Blue Turtle. Andy took all three of us for lunch today, and on the way, I thought 40 km/h felt like 100 km/h. After eating a delicious meal with good company, we drove home, and I was less afraid. The wind hitting our faces helped cool us down in the afternoon heat, which reached 91°F (33°C).

Many of the families from the Traveling Village live in the same resort, Banana Beach, and we are starting to find a rhythm. At times, living in a community feels overwhelming, but at others, it feels just right. Morning and evening are the best times for me to play near the ocean and visit with others in the resort's restaurant.

I find myself comparing this to Vietnam and missing certain parts of it. This location is more of a challenge for me because of the heat, and I'm not big into ocean sports. The bar soap scents here are wild. I spent some time in three different shops using Google Translate to find an unscented bar, and after trying three that all offended my nose, I am trying an online website called Lazada (it is like Amazon for Asia) to order a few products. The turmeric I love to cook with doesn't sound like a good idea for soap, especially since I handwash my clothes and don't want to stain my white garments.

The Thai Baht is about 30 to 1 USD, and they have coins here. In Vietnam, 1 USD was worth 25,000 Vietnamese Dong, and there were no coins; only paper money.

I am making a personal goal to do the following things while in Thailand:
*Drink/eat one fresh coconut a day
*Try a new Thai food 5 out of 7 days of the week
*Sketch/draw for at least 15 minutes a day

Andy, Ani, and Irene on the Blue Turtle Scooter

Sunset in Koh Lanta

March 4th
Koh Lanta, Thailand – first week complete

Sure enough, I can tolerate staying outside in the afternoon heat one week into my time here. The Traveling Village Calendar was so quiet at the beginning of last week and is now brimming with possible things to participate in. Because Ani feels safe here at our lodging among so many other families, Andy and I have been able to do things together. We have always been drawn to being active together (we met through unicycling), and now we run together at 7 am several days a week. Today we tried a covered football (soccer) field and played with six other kids and adults from the village. There are also several types of yoga classes being hosted by community members. I participated in my first laughter yoga session last Wednesday. I was delighted to discover that the guided laughter exercises led to genuine belly laughs, which released oxytocin and other beneficial hormones.

We purchased an inflatable stand-up paddleboard that arrived this afternoon. We plan to take it out this evening for our first paddle.

One village member, Martin, wants to relaunch his coaching career, so he has created quick, gym-based weight-training routines for adults who want to stay in shape but have limited time. He calls it "Papa Power Hour," and several Mamas have joined. I enjoy the challenge of learning to use weights to maintain mobility and change my memories of going to the gym into something sustainable. The last time I was actively lifting weights was during my first year of college, when I was on the crew team, and we would wake up at 5 am for weight training. I didn't enjoy doing it then.

Another mother uses a group of 12 of us to test a healing method and equip us with tools to calm our nervous systems. I joined this small group and appreciate it, as it allows me to focus on my growth while also hearing about others' struggles.

I spoke with a mother in our village over breakfast, and she helped me see that there aren't many natural resources we can tap into here in Koh Lanta. The land almost feels like it has too many tourists. We are searching for ways to connect with this place. I think that, due to this lack of abundance in nature, I am inclined to turn to the members of the village as our primary resource. Today, Giuseppe hosted a beginning coding class for the children, and about 12 kids showed up to learn the basics of coding in Scratch. There is a wealth of knowledge among the people. This month, I am focusing on getting to know other families better and having meaningful conversations as time allows. I was delighted yesterday when J, a two-year-old boy, took my hand for the first time and walked me to breakfast. We had been greeting each other daily while staying at our lodging in Vietnam, and although his primary language is Dutch, friendliness is universal.

Favorite foods this week:
Green Curry (although it is almost too spicy for me!)
Massaman Curry
Mango sticky rice
Fresh coconuts

Jellyfish

Irene and Ani swimming at our friend's pool

March 9th

Here is a summary from this past week:

Positive moments:
*I learned how to use a motor scooter and drive it successfully for the first time.
*We are living close to 15 other families and have easy access to conversations and friendship
*The food in Thailand is delicious. The other night, I had a yellow curry that made me want to savor every bite.
*I've been doing Papa Power Hour Workouts with Martin and several other village members at a gym, making me feel more comfortable in a gym setting and helping me gain strength.
*The Stand Up Paddle Board is fun to use, and the access point is convenient, with the beach close to our lodging.
*I appreciate having breakfast made for us and daily room service to make the beds and change the towels. I feel fortunate not to have to manage these things right now.
*We visited the Koh Lanta Animal Welfare for a tour last week. It is one of the nicer animal shelters I have ever seen. They have well-thought-out systems, ample space for the dogs to run, and beautiful art on the shelter's walls. I can tell there is much care and love put into this place.

Challenges:
*Visiting the Animal Welfare shelter made Ani feel strongly about wanting to own a pet and have her own room to settle down in. We continue this conversation to find a solution that works for the whole family, but it isn't easy.
*The heat makes me feel very lethargic, and I've had a few headaches from the heat this past week. Siesta in the afternoons helps make living here possible.
*Jellyfish are abundant in the ocean, making ocean swimming challenging without getting stung. This makes Stand-up Paddleboarding more of an adventurous sport! Andy went further out and said he was counting the jellyfish, but stopped after 40.

*The pool has had a few children pooping in it, which has led to more chemicals being put in it, which has led to several kids getting chemical rashes. It seems a bit ironic that we are so close to the water, yet I don't feel comfortable swimming in either the ocean or the pool.

*There is a high number of women who use prostitution to make a living. Some bars have beautiful women sitting in them by the roadside at night. I have also heard that there is a problem with child prostitution, which makes me feel nauseous.

*This is a highly touristy area, which makes me question being a tourist as well and how I can coexist here in a way that is helpful to the Thai people.

Ani and Irene

March 17th
What's good and challenging about this lifestyle this week

A highlight this week is not having to retell my travel story to new people. Traveling with the same group means conversations can go deeper instead of staying on the surface.

The older kids organized a mangrove kayaking outing, and I joined. I was paired with another single mother, and we enjoyed paddling together. We agreed we were glad we had not brought our children because they would not have enjoyed it.

The tour guide took us close to a "friendly" monkey family and even tried to lure a monkey onto his kayak. We paddled over to discourage him, but he ignored us. The monkey climbed onto his kayak and then onto someone else's.

Later, a different group of monkeys, the unfriendly kind, approached some kayaks near the shore. One grabbed a water bottle, and another swam toward a kayak and showed its teeth at a young boy. Thankfully no one was hurt, although it was intense. When the current became too strong, the guides called boats to pick us up. We held onto mangroves carefully, checking for monkeys before grabbing on.

Midway through our four-month Traveling Village, we held a beautiful celebration marking two months. We created a mandala with rocks, shells, and flowers. An artist in our group made natural paints from crushed stones, and faces looked like tribal warriors. Some shells were returned to the sea on a paddleboard as an offering.

The celebration continued with a sunset beach picnic. One family brought floating flower bundles for the kids to light and release with a wish. We watched a private fire show until a sudden downpour created a dramatic ending. The group scattered. Andy debated paddling back in the rain and dark and thankfully chose not to.

Ani went back with a friend, and I rode on the back of the motorbike holding a sandy, deflated paddleboard. That night I washed loads of sand from our clothes and backpack.

The Thai food continues to be a joy. Khao Soi with endless toppings, flavorful curries, and fresh coconuts every day.

We have fully embraced siestas.

Veggie Curry

Flowers and sea shells from the midway party

Sunset in Koh Lanta

March 18th

Today, Ani and I took it slow. Andy went snorkeling with a group of other Villagers. After the morning workout with Andrea, I showered and did laundry in our wash tub, stomping my feet while listening to music. I danced to a song in our room. I am participating in an adult group focused on calming the nervous system, and dancing daily is actually part of our 'own' work this week.

Ani and I went to Sam Batik in the walking market area of Koh Lanta to make our own sarongs. This time, we each made one. I am pleased with how mine turned out, and I appreciated how little Sam said. His manner of conduct is calm and methodical. Once he set us up, he said a few words, but mostly, he just let us create. What a treasure to find this open art studio amongst shops in a walking area.

I ate at The Garden Restaurant, watching koi fish swim under a waterfall while eating panang curry. I ordered a mild version, but still bit into some amazingly spicy red Thai chilis. My threshold for spicy food is increasing!

Ani creating a sarong

March 21st

Time For Lime

Today we participated in a private group cooking class with Time
For Lime, the first Thai cooking school in Koh Lanta. All proceeds
benefit the Lanta Animal Shelter, which was founded by Junie
Kovacs 21 years ago. She visited Koh Lanta, and at that time, she
said you couldn't walk safely on the beaches because of all of the
stray dogs. They have been working to spay and neuter as many
animals as possible over the years. The Thai Government has
collected stray dogs from the streets and beaches and put them
together in yards in several places around Thailand. Then they
throw food over the gate, as no one wants to go in there. I asked
Junie why they do this, and she said, "You ask me, and I ask you." It
makes no sense and only creates more puppies and worsens the
living conditions for the dogs already there. Every year, they try to
save some dogs from these yards and find them homes. The
puppies are always the easiest to rehome.

Today in the cooking class, we created delicious Thai food with
the help of the head chef, Noi, and several other staff members
who prepared some ingredients for us and cleaned up after us. I
asked Noi how he came to love cooking. He said he grew up in a
poor family, and when he was a teenager, his parents suggested it
would benefit their family if he agreed to become a monk at a
monastery. For six years, he lived in the monastery and cooked
there. I asked whether that monastery was vegetarian, and he said
no; they would accept whatever food the villagers could share
with them. He said that some monks will even mix all their food
(desserts, main dishes, salads) so they don't become attached to
the flavor of any one item. Where he lived, they didn't practice
this. I had never heard of this before. He and his staff are also in
their high season, and they sometimes do two cooking classes a
day, each lasting 5–6 hours. There is a low season when no tourists
come to Koh Lanta, so it isn't possible to work.

We learned the process for making green curry (using a mortar and pestle; it takes 45-60 minutes to mix the ingredients thoroughly). They had already prepared a curry for our cooking today, and we saw the ingredients, smelled the curry mix, and helped pound it with a pestle. Then we made fried spring rolls, stir-fried red curry paste with tofu, green curry, and fried rice. Green and red curry are very similar recipes. Massaman and panang curries are thicker and use different ingredients and spices. I have thorougly enjoyed eating so many curries here in Thailand these past few weeks, and am happy to finally know what ingredients are used to make them!

Irene and Ani at the Time For Lime cooking class

Fried rice with tom kah kai soup

Fried tofu with beans, rice, and spring roll

March 25th

I stepped out of my comfort zone twice this week, once by organizing a large group to attend a cooking class and another time by helping with a group Film Festival project. There were times over the past few days when I felt like I was back in college, living in the dorms. There was so much activity going on around me that I didn't want to miss out on, yet at times I longed for quiet to rejuvenate.

One of the sweetest things about communal living has been getting to know other people's children. I have a little friend, age 1, named Jo, who only uses about four words, and one of them is Irene. It is so sweet, it melts my heart every time. Last night at the film festival, as we were all sitting together watching the short films that the children and adults had put together these past few days, Jo's little hand appeared from behind my right shoulder with a piece of popcorn in it for me to eat. I gratefully accepted, and then he continued feeding me popcorn and chunks of watermelon as the evening went on. For all the swirling feelings of being out of balance and doing too much, this simple experience of connecting with a one-year-old and feeling a part of the village made up for it.

We haven't thrived in the heat, and I struggle to know when to push Ani to step out of her comfort zone. We took today really slow, and we are all looking forward to the temperature change that will be with us in Japan starting on April 3rd.

March 29th
This past week in Koh Lanta

I went to a leaf printing class with my friend Marie. It was a fun class, led by a Thai woman named Yanitha. She has a passion for this, and even though her hands are sensitive to leaves (she wore gloves to avoid provoking her sensitivity), she continues with this art form. The prints turned out beautiful. The colors are so vibrant, which is a surprise as the leaves all seemed to be a similar shade of green as we laid them out on the fabric.

I went to a CrossFit Box Gym here in Koh Lanta with Martin and several other Traveling Village Members to do a workout that Martin created for us participants in his Papa Power Hour Program. I almost got my toes to the bar, which is a goal of mine. I never thought I would go to a CrossFit gym, but here I am typing this!

That same night, I was ill, throwing up three times, I think, because of food poisoning. I'm not sure what I was sick from, but it sure knocked me out for a good 24 hours.

I didn't leave our room except to sit on the balcony for the rest of the next day.
Ani doesn't want to leave the room often because of the heat. It isn't common to find places to eat with air conditioning here on the island, so sometimes we eat in our room with the air conditioning on, then I clean up well after ourselves so we don't attract ants.

Ani and I made a sand castle together and decorated the top with shells.

I am thriving with the Traveling Village, and also very much looking forward to five days of travel alone with just our family to regroup and reconnect. I feel like we have been scattered here, with so many interactions and activities to choose from.

Leaf prints made by Irene and Marie   66

April 1st

Our last days on the island of Koh Lanta, Thailand

I visited the Following Giants Elephant Sanctuary on my own on Sunday afternoon. Going alone meant I connected with other people who were also signed up for the tour that day. I explained why I was in Koh Lanta for five weeks with the Traveling Village and what I did during that time to a family from northern England who were visiting Koh Lanta for two days during an Easter holiday trip. It gave me a nice reframing of my life in the village and helped me realize how nice it is to live life with others while traveling together. Quite a few of our activities weren't specific to Koh Lanta: like playing soccer/football twice a week together, following a gym program with Martin and Andrea, frequent beach runs with Giuseppe and Andy, and the weekly parenting group. They were activities and things we did as a village, which you cannot find by searching Google or TripAdvisor.

At Following Giants, we did just that: we followed five elephants as they led their everyday lives. We learned so much about their behavior from our guide. A mahout is assigned to each elephant to follow it and care for it. The elephant takes 1–3 years to fully bond with its mahout and recognize its mahout's scent. Typically, this position is filled by a man, though in northern Thailand, among native tribes, women serve as mahouts. This position is passed down through family lines; there isn't a school to attend to learn how to become one. One mahout had to go to the hospital, and after a few days, the elephant became worried. They actually used Zoom to communicate from the hospital to the elephant, so it knew the mahout was OK and would return. Substitute mahouts are available for occasional vacations or emergencies. I was in wonder watching these beautiful animals move around, eat, and bathe. This place had a history of elephant riding, but it has since become an ethical sanctuary where the elephants are not touched or forced to perform. Elephants need to walk around 6 miles a day to remain healthy.

I didn't have anything prepared adequately for Easter this year, but other adults in the village pulled together an Easter Egg Hunt on Sunday at 11 am. The children drew an egg, and the adults hid it. Once they found their paper egg, they turned it in for a Kinder Egg. The heat here has really made me feel like I can work at half capacity, and the idea of hiding chocolate or candies in the sun and heat was not appealing, so I am thankful they came together in this way.

Following Giants Elephant Sanctuary

THAILAND to SINGAPORE

April 5th

Krabi, Thailand – after a delicious lunch at the base of our Family Tree Hotel, we took a siesta to wait out the heat of the day. We explored the city with several other families, including a visit to a Buddhist temple. Ani was hungry, so we left the group and ate sushi together. She didn't fully unpack her bag, as we were only staying one night in Krabi. At 9:45 pm, Ani realized she had lost her finger panda, Banbaleena (BB), and couldn't find her! A search ensued, and then fears that she had left her at the sushi restaurant, which closed at 9 pm and reopened the following day, hours after we were scheduled to depart. Ani has brought BB everywhere with her since she bought it at the Chinese Garden in Portland last July. She was heartbroken. I did my best to comfort her, creating all kinds of pretend stories with imaginary friends, then ending with real–life stories about losing dogs I loved and the feelings that came with them. She finally fell asleep after listening to a guided 61–point meditation, close to midnight. We awoke at 5 am to catch our flight to Singapore and were in pretty low spirits, knowing we would likely be leaving BB behind in Thailand.

Nritya, who was with us in Krabi, suggested I reach out to Marie and another family departing from Krabi later that day. I sent many text messages, and after landing in Singapore, I tried calling the Thai sushi restaurant only to discover they don't answer their phone. No website, no FB page, and we decided that she was gone. I thanked Marie, who had offered to help bring her to us in Japan if I could get a hold of the restaurant to confirm whether she was there and arrange for her to be delivered to her residence in Thailand. I was reminded of a book by Mo Willems called "Knuffle Bunny," where his daughter leaves her beloved stuffed rabbit on the plane on their trip to the Netherlands. We continued in Singapore, reassuring Ani that we could find another finger panda. After online searching, I discovered the pandas are actually marketed as refrigerator magnets and are available on Amazon.

We went slowly because of the heat, fatigue, and bummed-out feelings around BB. We visited the Art and Science Museum, which is shaped like a flower. Deciding to eat before buying tickets, we went to the food court at the Sands Bay Marina Mall next door. Inside, there was a fantastic food court and an interactive art exhibition by Team Borderless in the mall's central area. We ate some food, and then Ani and I paid to enter and participate in the art activity. Using templates, you colored in a flower or animal, then they scanned it, and it came to life on the giant floor in front of you. You could chase your art piece around and jump on it. I loved seeing Ani run and smile. We returned to the Art and Science Museum and decided that touring the free areas was enough for us this time. We walked and took the metro to our hotel for the night, The Clan Hotel. This hotel is one of the nicest I have ever stayed in. There was a filtered water tap in the room! The bed felt like a cloud! The toilet had an interactive heated seat! A rain shower! A tea ceremony was included in our visit! Plus a rooftop pool.

Singapore is a clean city. Chewing gum is illegal, and you notice the streets are very well kept. There are signs everywhere listing the fines one can incur for not following the rules, such as eating on the metro or parking a motorcycle incorrectly. After eating at a local Hawker Center (large food court), we returned to our hotel. Ani and I decided to go swimming, and as she went to grab her swimsuit from her suitcase, she discovered her finger panda, BB, wrapped up in her swimsuit! We all stared in disbelief, having mourned this little panda all day, then Ani cried tears of joy, and I gave Ani a big hug. Somehow, she put her in her partially opened suitcase the night before and couldn't find her when we searched everywhere in the hotel room. I sent a bunch of messages to the families I had previously alerted about her search, and they were all so happy to hear the news.

We slept well in a king bed that didn't even squeak when we turned over. The room didn't have mosquitoes, a musty smell, or sewer fumes.

To ride the metro, you simply tap your phone to enter, as it is linked to your credit card. Andy would tap his phone to let Ani through, then switch cards in his Google Wallet and tap again to get through. Tapping the machines upon exiting charges your card the correct amount based on the distance you traveled. Each metro stop was numbered. There was an announcement before each stop that said, "Mind the gap, and be happy happy when you go on the platform." There was a monitor showing videos on what to do in emergencies. One was about being molested, and it had the words "crime against modesty" at the end. They were done very tastefully so that all ages could watch.

Ani waiting for the public transportation to arrive

Irene and Ani in the Team Borderless Exhibit.

An example of a fine in Singapore

Walking to the Art and Science Museum

TOKYO, JAPAN

April 7th

Every day we were able to meet up with at least one friend, which made me feel so happy and connected. Day 1, we visited a hedgehog cafe and ended up enjoying the company of Tara, the Tenrec, and the small panda mice the most. In the evening, we saw Beau Hoover, a long-time unicycle friend. After meeting him for pizza, I joined him at a two-hour meditation meetup where we did a guided meditation, had tea, and shared in a circle. I miss regular sitting meditation sessions with others, so this was fulfilling.

On day 2, we visited the TeamLab Borderless digital art museum. For the first hour, I was in awe as the art moved from one room to the next, and I could interact with the art pieces by touching the walls. However, the last 45 minutes became too much for me, and eventually, I just wanted to get out because I was starting to feel seasick. We ate at a ramen restaurant, where you purchase soup at a ticket machine.
After a nap to help my brain unscramble from the art and my stomach digest the heavy ramen soup, we met up with Satomi, a unicycle friend who lives in Tokyo. She has a 2-year-old daughter, A, who is super sweet. We ate dinner together at an Alice in Wonderland-themed restaurant. The last time we saw Satomi was when she and her sister performed in Cirque Du Soleil's Amaluna in Winnipeg, Canada. Andy worked closely with her mother, Mayumi, to organize the International Unicycling Competition UNICON in Tokyo in 2004.

Day 3: We went to Harajuku to meet my friend Myla and her family, who were in Japan this week, too. We hugged and shared a few moments before going our separate ways. Myla suggested checking out a nearby capsule store, and Ani loved browsing all the miniature options.

Satomi asked her friend for a few bicycle shop recommendations so that I could bring my unicycle to have the spokes tightened.

I took the metro on Saturday afternoon to one whose owner was a unicyclist, thinking that would be my best chance at finding a good wheel builder. I arrived and looked at the owner, and with a flash of recognition between us, he said, "Andy wife!" I said, "Yes! Andy's wife! Irene." It turns out it is Takuji-san, or Tak, a unicyclist who has even traveled to the US for Moab Muni fest, and he has visited our farm before as well. We were all three surprised, Satomi, Tak, and I. Tak was kind enough to fix my wheel for free, and now it rides beautifully without squeaking. I rode home 8 miles, all the while smiling and amazed at the connection that just happened here in Japan. The people I have met through unicycling are so kind and friendly.

Tokyo's subway system, the Tokyo Metro, is often considered one of the world's most efficient, clean, and punctual systems. It is also known for its extensive coverage, with over 300 stations and multiple lines connecting all major city areas. It is truly a wonder. The subway system goes multiple levels underground, and we walked many miles and climbed many stairs during our four days there.

Enjoying craft soymilk in Tokyo

Shibuya scramble crossing

Cherry blossoms at night

Art by Ani for Satomi

KYOTO, JAPAN

April 11th

Toilets in Japan –
I'd like to highlight how nice the toilets are in Japan. We visited a
park in Kyoto yesterday to see the beautiful cherry blossoms, and
even in a crowded park, the bathroom facilities are clean, have
heated seats, bidet features, and some will start to play sounds of
a waterfall or bird song for you when you sit down on the seat to
cover up any noise. At a mall a few days ago, I entered the
bathroom and saw a beautiful room for mothers to nurse or pump.
Many women's bathrooms have small urinals for mothers with
young boys. All public restrooms are free.

Public transportation in Japan –
We have been taking the bus frequently in Kyoto over the past few
days. On a packed bus, it is always very quiet. People are so good
about standing up to offer their seat to an elderly person or a
mother with a child. Only once in the six or so times I've been on
the bus have I felt slightly uncomfortable, and that was simply
because many people were making me feel cramped. Even still, at
our stop, we went from the back of a packed bus to the front to
pay the driver as we exited. The driver waited for us to approach
as everyone leaned in to make space for us to exit through the
front of the bus.

Remembering the power of nature in Japan –
My favorite parenting book, *Hunt, Gather, Parent*, suggests that
when a child is in a bad mood, bringing them outdoors to focus on
nature can help. Yesterday I used this advice and took a certain
child to a stream, where the sound of the water and the falling
cherry petals helped her get out of her funk. We spent the entire
afternoon outside enjoying the warm weather, beautiful cherry
blossoms, and friends from the Traveling Village.

Ani and Silja in a stream with cherry petals around them

Ani's finger panda, BB, enjoying the cherry blossoms

Irene and Andy in Maruyama Park

Iris flower in Maruyama Park

April 13th

This rainbow pancake cake, created in the shared kitchen of the
Fujitaya Hostel, is the second rainbow pancake cake we have
made abroad. The first was created in a shared hostel kitchen in
the Galapagos Islands.

Irene and Ani with the rainbow pancake
cake with avocado chocolate frosting

The rainbow pancakes were created
using food coloring and cooked on the
stove top before being put together.

April 14th

Today, we met Tricia Kiewel and Aurora Lent (@aurora.wandering)
in Kyoto, Japan!

Tricia and Aurora were some of Ani's first caretakers when we all
lived in Hutchinson and needed help with our farm. They have also
helped us demolish lath-and-plaster walls, plant trees, weed
strawberry fields, pick so many tomatoes, and be overall excellent
cheerleaders for us in so many ways.

Aurora, Tricia, Andy, and Ani

Irene, Aurora, and Tricia

April 16th

These past five days in Kyoto:

We are starting to find our rhythm in community life here at our hostel. Six other families from the Traveling Village are staying at the same hostel. Because everyone is further apart here, we have spent more time on buses and the metro than we did in Thailand getting to communal meals and gatherings.

We have had some great days and some challenging ones. The challenging one reminded me that we need to slow down and remember to live, not just try to do. Slow activities that have felt nourishing to me include:
*Making a rainbow pancake cake with Ani with chocolate avocado maple syrup frosting and sharing it with whoever was in the community space at our hostel
*Purposely choosing only to do one thing a day with Ani, so that we have plenty of downtime to regenerate.
*Sharing breakfast with other Traveling Village families in the communal kitchen these past two mornings. Leheng had the good idea to try eating breakfast together and went out to buy a bunch of groceries for us. He created an overnight spinach, chia seed, almond-milk pudding that he served over yogurt, with crepes and blueberry/banana pancakes, and on toasts with basil pesto, peppers, tomatoes, and melted cheese. We made a few things dairy-free so I could enjoy them too, and it was lovely. With the leftover bread and eggs, we had a French Toast breakfast together this morning.

Irene, Andy, and Giuseppe on a morning run. A temple is in the background.

Some of our outings this week included:
*Visiting a pug dog cafe with Ani. I don't know how I feel about it, as there were good and kind of crazy parts, but in the end, I'm glad we had the experience, and I don't need to do it again.
*Participating in a book-making class using Kimono fabric. This was incredible: a master bookbinder taught the class, and it was like a well-oiled machine, with us putting together the most beautiful sketchbooks.
*Andy and I went running in the mornings, sometimes with our friend Giuseppe, and once I went alone. We are preparing for a trail race on May 11th, to be held here in Japan.
*Communal meals
*Playground meet-ups

Bookbinding cover possibilities with different kimono fabrics

April 21st

We have taken many buses and metro rides to get to places around Kyoto. The buses remain comfortable to ride; people are quiet and polite, offering free seats to the elderly, the young, and anyone who might seem older than they are. On one bus ride, a woman tried asking Ani how old she was, and we said, "Nine." She moved something around in her purse, and once it was our stop and Ani had walked past her, the woman offered me a small new bag of candies for Ani. I graciously accepted and walked off the bus with a pleasant feeling of how the Japanese revere children.

I've tried bodyweight workouts in our hostel room, which are challenging given the limited space. However, I have managed to do some sit-ups on our thin sleeping mat, and that feels good.

I made spring vegetable soup for many members of our hostel group. However, I realized that we don't have very big pots and pans, so I may need to make it in two batches for the next meal.

I tried to welcome downtime at our hostel and in our room, as living communally requires a lot of energy from me.

Spent time researching Airbnb and Booking.com for lodging in Japan after the Traveling Village is over. I'm new to Booking.com and have found it interesting to compare the same properties across both platforms, examine price differences, and get a feel for the review system.

April 25th

Today I went for my longest training run, 14.8 miles with 1,972 ft of elevation gain. Andy and I woke up early to catch a train a few stops east into the hills, and then ran together for 7.5 miles. He hopped on a train so he could get back in time for an event he helped organize at 12 pm. I ran home. This is the longest run I've done since becoming a mother. I am grateful for the Traveling Village community and our hostel, and Ani being old enough to feel comfortable being left home alone for a few hours while we go exercise together. I felt good and hope to stay healthy and have an enjoyable run on May 11th.

We have just over two weeks left with the Traveling Village. We have learned so much about ourselves, communal living, the cultures we have visited, and the cultures we represent, drawn from the countries we all come from.

Drawing by Ani

On a long run with Andy

April 30th

I have been reflecting on things that happen that I am not showing in photos or videos in my updates. I have been living life, constantly trying to return to what I want my life to look like, free from comparisons or from what another family is doing. I have to keep finding my way to maintain balance so I can show up for my family, community, and the human race. I have to say no and be OK with missing out on what those around me may be doing at that moment or day.

I spend a lot of time using Google Translate to read labels when at the grocery store. I use it to ask about ingredients in menu items, and to communicate with a bicycle store owner to replace the tube on my unicycle. I used it to ask a grocery clerk if they sold large bars of dark chocolate for baking, then followed three kind Japanese men around the store while they tried to help me, all while bowing in respect and service. This large grocery store didn't sell large bars; the large size seems to be a thing from the West. This same store sells asparagus stalks neatly packaged with three stalks in a package, because why would you want to buy more at once? Andy took a gallon-sized (about four liters) ziplock bag to a refillable store to fill it up with oatmeal. He said at least three people helping him in the store asked him why he wanted so much oatmeal. When he brought it back to our hostel, the hostel owners looked at the bag in surprise, because large bags of that size of oatmeal aren't sold here in Japan. The hostel owners took our photo with the bag to remember this strange purchase!

The music in grocery stores is often classical or upbeat, or a whistling soundtrack, which makes you feel relaxed while shopping. I love the ready-to-eat baked or roasted sweet potatoes at the grocery and convenience stores. After using Google Translate, I realized that one store even sells organic and conventional sweet potatoes.

We continue to train for our upcoming trail run on May 11th. Andy and I are sore every day. The other day, I took a two-hour nap in the afternoon and slept through the night, as my body needed the rest. The Traveling Village is very active, with American soccer/football practice twice a week, bodyweight workouts, and even an outing to a bouldering gym this week.

When I see Geishas on the street, I admire them but don't take their pictures (as it isn't allowed). I looked at YouTube to see if I'd like to bring Ani to a show, but I realized this art form isn't for me. I sighed, feeling somehow wrong for not loving everything everyone else seems to love. Then, I remembered to come back to myself. We can still learn about them without going to a show.

Japanese lunch

Andy doing a bodyweight workout

May 1st

--- F I V E Y E A R S S L O W T R A V E L I N G ---

Today marks five years since we left our farm in Hutchinson, Minnesota, and began this slow-traveling lifestyle. In these five years, we have visited 28 countries, 23 states, and all 10 Canadian provinces. Often, people ask me, "Do you have a favorite country that you've visited?" I don't have a specific place; much of our experience and memory is shaped by the people we meet there. I can share that the most extended length of time we have stayed in one place so far is Japan (with our estimated departure date of June 28th), followed by Ecuador (we went back several times to stay at Punta La Barca), Canada (all 10 provinces were done in the first year of our travels when we moved at a quicker pace), Portugal (while participating in Boundless Life), and Croatia (exploring the beauty of this country and appreciating being outside of the Schengen area during our year in Europe).

We still don't know where we want to land permanently. This topic comes up often, and we look forward to connecting with our Midwest friends and family this summer. However, Andy and I want to travel again this winter, and we'll see how Ani feels after being back in Minnesota for a few months.

May 5th

I went to a public bath this week. Public bath houses are called sentos in Japanese. I went into the entrance, took off my shoes, and locked them in a locker. Then I went into the first door I saw and saw a full frontal view of a naked man walking out of the men's bathing area. I looked to my right and saw an older woman at the check-in counter. She saw my mistake and motioned me out to enter through the women's door. Then I entered and explained, using Google Translate, that it was my first time. She understood and, with a smile, accepted my coins to enter. I undressed, took a stool, and washed up while sitting, then enjoyed the hot pools there. Next time I would also tie my hair up, as I realize now that is proper etiquette, to keep hair from getting in the clean water of the hot baths.

There were also saunas available. It was a pleasant experience, and I left feeling warm through and through.

I also experienced a kaiseki meal with five other adults from the Traveling Village. Kaiseki is a traditional multi-course Japanese dinner composed of dozens of small dishes with varied flavors and textures. It is considered the most refined form of washoku (Japanese cuisine), which UNESCO designated as Intangible Cultural Heritage. There were several courses with different flavors that I usually wouldn't order, but I was pleased to try them with others. My favorite dish was the udon noodle soup, with soft, crisp noodles and a few slivers of wagyu beef on top. I also enjoyed the simple jelly dessert of matcha mochi with fresh strawberries.

Andy organized one last event where we gathered as a group and used communal funds to buy chopsticks at a chopstick store (we even had our names engraved on them!). Then we walked through the walking streets, snacking at several different spots along the way. The onigiri (Japanese rice balls) were the first stop, then edamame, then honey ice cream, and we finished with another gelato/sweets store. Interestingly, since then, both Andy and I have decided to take this week without eating refined sugar, as we feel like we have been indulging too often here in Japan. It is also a nice detox leading up to our race/run next Saturday.

May 9th

Little Heaven Vegan Restaurant

I sent three emails to arrange a date and time to dine. The last one asked, "Do you want to pre-order the vegan sushi plate? It is by reservation only." I responded with a resounding "yes!"

I arrived today, 10 minutes before my solo reservation, having learned that I enjoy nice vegan restaurants more on my own than in a family setting. The restaurant could seat 16 people, but today I was the only one in the whole place. A kind waiter greeted me and led me to my seat, next to a sliding glass door, where tiny potted Japanese maples outside were being gently tussled by the wind. The place was perfectly in order, with calming music playing. The waiter carefully arranged my placemat and took my drink order for herbal tea. I waited quietly, watching the greenery outside and trying to make a photo memory of this experience. I had witnessed other solo diners at Japanese restaurants sitting patiently, not using their phones or other devices, seemingly meditating as they waited to be served. The waiter served me an impressive vegan sushi tray. The 'salmon' was a poached tomato that looked so impressive that only my taste buds gave away that it wasn't fish. I enjoyed every piece of sushi, sometimes closing my eyes to focus on the flavor combinations. I looked to my right and saw a black head disappear into the kitchen. That was when I realized the waiter was quietly checking on me, timing his service perfectly so as not to interrupt my meal or experience. When I had finished, he came back out and, after praising the sushi, I ordered the soba tasting dish, which came with two kinds of soba – one cold and one hot- to taste. I dipped the cold soba into the broth, made from shiitake mushrooms and kelp, and added shaved green onions and a touch of wasabi. Then I ate the noodles so they wouldn't get too soggy, sitting in the broth on their own. The sound of the sliding door to the kitchen made me realize that the waiter was politely checking in on me again. I smiled.

He cleared my plate and served me the hot soba with a piece of tofu on top.

At the end, he brought out the Soba-yu, the water the soba noodles had been cooked in, which contained the nutrients from the soba, and encouraged me to mix it with the dipping sauce and taste.

After paying the bill and using the washroom, I went outside to my bicycle. Again, the waiter met me at the door and bowed in appreciation as he wished me farewell. I feel like this was a lovely Japanese experience, carefully considered and cared for throughout the five days leading up to my meal and time in the restaurant.

I admire how conscientious Japanese people are of others.

The vegan sushi plate

The Japanese maple I admired

May 11th

We did it! Five of us completed the 23 km Mt. Hiei International Trail Run today. It was the first trail-running race for both Andy and me. Kudos to Andy for running and hiking alongside me, and for sharing a salt pill when my brain started to feel scrambled from the exertion and sweat. About ten minutes after taking it, I felt much better, and I stopped imagining the words coming out of his mouth as actual visual objects. I was close to bonking, but not quite.

Noodle break during the race. They also had fermented foods, sweet potatoes, and eggs

Doing the trail run with others from the Traveling Village made the experience even more meaningful. Training for this race was possible because we stayed in each location long enough to run regularly and get familiar with the roads. Having training buddies and a community that supported our family so that both Andy and I could participate was incredible. Some of my best memories from Kyoto came from those training runs.

Andy and I at the starting line for the run

Rocks placed to honour ancestors

May 14th

The Traveling Village ended today. As I write this, we are on a Shinkansen (bullet train) to Hiroshima. There, we can meet up with a few other families from the TV.

I am aware of holding all these feelings at once: sadness, happiness, delight, loneliness, longing, questioning of purpose, and more.

Highlights from the past week:
*Going to Vegan Ramen UZU in Kyoto. A Bib Gourmand accolade Restaurant in the MICHELIN Guide. We ate with Nanna and Andy and shared bites from our meals. I ordered the Mountain Herbs Ramen, and the spice stretched my taste buds, then cooled as my mouth chewed on fiddlehead ferns, greens, and edible flowers.
*Remembering the sweetness that comes from co-living with others. After recharging in my room, I could come out and be social; I didn't have to arrange a meetup. During the hard times of co-living, having others to talk with about my feelings and knowing that I could ask for boundaries to be set made things better.

Mountain Herbs Ramen

Sushi appetizer

HIROSHIMA, JAPAN

May 16th

This city is the first military target of a nuclear weapon in history. Andy and I walked through the Peace Museum on our own to learn more about the history of this event. We spoke with Ani about it, and I showed her some photos from the museum as well. The city was demolished, except for the Hiroshima Prefectural Industrial Promotion Hall, now commonly known as the Atomic Bomb Dome, which stands in Hiroshima Peace Memorial Park. Because this town was rebuilt after 1945, the streets are more expansive and have a modern feel. After going through the museum, I felt very heavy and sad. There are busloads of Japanese children who come to the Peace Memorial Park to see the museum and all of the statues and monuments that have been erected for Peace so that there will never be another bomb dropped again. Looking at the children, most appeared to be middle school-aged or older.

Giuseppe went for one last run with Andy this morning, then visited the museum and met up with me for another run. Since we aren't living with other families in a co-living situation at the moment, I didn't feel right about leaving Ani alone in the apartment, so Giuseppe made two last runs with our family. It helped us so much to have another friend as a running buddy these past months, knowing that Giuseppe was waiting for us to get up and out the door.

Ani and I visited a mini pig cafe this afternoon. It was one of the best pet cafe experiences we've had, as they didn't feed the animals anything, and the pigs were friendly. They wanted to dig with their noses, with one larger pig digging along the outside of my right leg, giving me a strange leg massage, then piled on top of us to get the 'best' place. There was a cute pink pig that just wanted to be cuddled right next to your head, and she chose Ani, which made Ani's afternoon.

This evening, we had dinner with several families from the Traveling Village and said our final goodbyes. It was sad walking home, but we felt hopeful our paths would cross again.

Atomic Bomb Dome

Ani with the sweet pig at the pig cafe

FUKUOKA, JAPAN –

May 19th

I went for a run yesterday morning and noticed palm trees lining some of the streets. They are neatly trimmed, with the trimmed area beneath the leaves wrapped in a bandage. I had to smile as things are kept so tidy and lovely here in Japan; it even shows on the palm trees. While running, I had to stop often to check my route, and I appreciated how aware drivers are of pedestrians. Sometimes the drivers would slow to a stop before proceeding through the intersection just to be sure they knew which crosswalk direction I would take. It feels like most people in Japan have a good sense of their bodies in space and take care not to bump into you on the street or on public transportation.

Yesterday, for lunch, we couldn't get Ani excited to go out to eat. Eventually, we got her out of the hostel, then decided to play rock-paper-scissors to see who got to choose where we ate lunch. Ani won two rounds, and she decided on a nice-looking grocery store. We went there, and then I went by myself to get some warm dumplings.

Today, we visited Ramen Stadium, a food court on the 5th floor of Canal City, featuring eight top-tier ramen restaurants. Then we got Ani a larger pair of shoes. I went for a walk on my own to explore a route through Fukuoka that AllTrails had created as an urban hike. It ended at Ohori Park on the lake. I saw many turtles swimming in the lake, along with birds and fish. It felt good to wander through the bustling city of Fukuoka. There are so many tall buildings and shopping areas with walking streets.

The change of pace from Traveling Village life is a challenge. I welcome the slower pace and fewer relationships to manage, even as I miss it all at the same time. I've reached out to other family and friends, and even had some time to create art with Ani and start a new book together. The book is titled *Out of My Mind* and follows a 10-year-old girl with cerebral palsy. It is well-written. We are taking some time to book the next leg of our journey in Japan. We try to plan, realize we need to wait, then talk about planning more, only to come back to waiting.

Andy and Ani on a walking street

Delicious dumplings!

May 21st

Today, we met up with Tricia (@jingletherapist) and Lilli (@lilli_anne_is_my_first_name) here in Fukuoka, Japan.

We had lunch at a sushi restaurant, then came back to the hostel to visit, and ended up playing Charades! I laughed until tears came to my eyes several times.

Tricia and Lilli both helped us a lot at York Farm when we were growing fruit and needed labor and childcare. Now Tricia lives in Japan, and we were able to see Lilli as she is visiting her mom for the summer.

Dragon character made by Ani during our stay in Fukuoka

Irene, Lilli, Tricia, Andy, and Ani

Ani playing Charades!

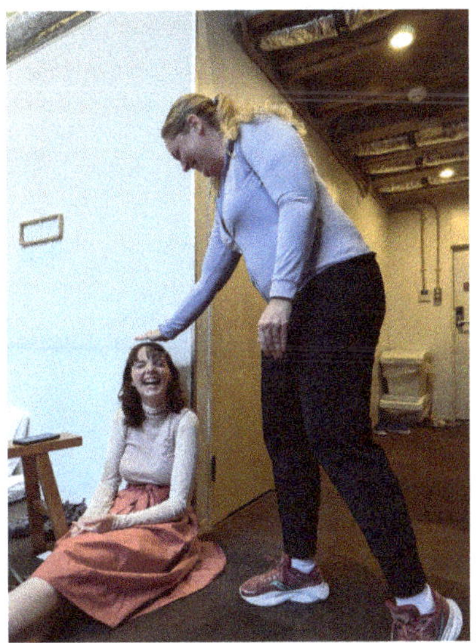

Lilli and Tricia playing Charades!

May 22nd

Bowing in Japan –
Having studied Buddhism and learned to bow in reverence to the Buddha, monks, and those in attendance at meditation sessions, I thought I would be prepared for bowing here in Japan. The culture here is so courteous toward one another and toward customers entering the stores. I feel like the experience is opening my eyes and helping me become even better at bowing in reverence to others. When checking out at a supermarket, if you go through a line with a clerk, they will bow when you reach the front, check out your items, thank you several times, then bow deeply as you pay and take your basket to leave. When you enter a restaurant or café, the staff will bow in acknowledgement of your presence, and again as you check out and exit the establishment. I find the practice very kind, and I also like it as an affirmation of your presence, knowing that you are seen and appreciated.

Adjusting to a slower-paced life –
Andy is getting over a bad cold; we all caught it just as the Traveling Village ended. I ran the 23km race with it, too. Now that it is just our family, our bodies are taking time to recuperate and rejuvenate after the fast-paced community living we experienced. In the morning, I find myself longing for human connection and feeling sad that it's over. The young children who used to wake us up when we co-lived aren't around anymore, and we're sleeping later. At first, it was a relief, but now it's a bit of a struggle to get back into an early rhythm and find our new routine. I'm reminding myself to appreciate this quieter time and make the most of our family-only time together. Ani and I enjoyed connecting over art and audiobooks this afternoon. I've found a couple of artists on Instagram who have inspired me to paint. @RebelUnicornCrafts is one of them.

I still haven't decided which race to train for, but I am trying to eat something green every day leading up to my 40th birthday. Sometimes it's a struggle, since we don't have a hot plate or an oven in our little kitchenette at the hostel. So far, I've found avocados, cucumbers, pickled greens, and seaweed to fill this goal. I've been going on runs here in Fukuoka and trying to keep my patience as I stop frequently to take in the scenery. Today, I ran to Ohori Lake and back with minimal checking, and I was happy that five miles went by without feeling like I had used up all my strength in my legs.

Unicycling by the Andy store

May 23rd

Yesterday we had a delightful cooking class with Hiroko at her home in Fukuoka, Japan. We learned how to make miso, then prepared lunch and ate together.

I discovered her cooking class through Airbnb Experiences. Past guests who participated said it was a unique, one-of-a-kind experience, and I couldn't agree more.

Some of the food came from her family's farm. We had cooked rice and miso-covered potatoes, with the rice and new potatoes coming from her family. She served delicious green tea at the end. It was so flavorful—almost like sweet grass with a hint of matcha. When I drank it, I felt like I was outside, smelling green grass around me.

Miso

Ani making an egg roll

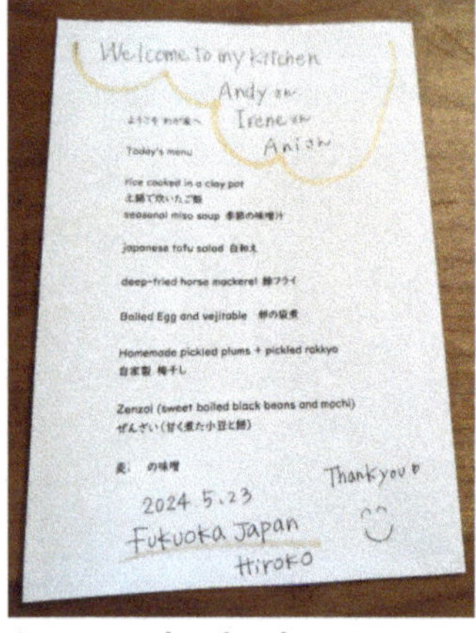

Our menu for the day

Lunch with Hiroko!

May 24th

Fear of Missing Out - FOMO -

We are slow travelers whose lives consist of constant, slow movement. It is a different way to approach seeing new places, and requires a different mindset. Instead of cramming all the sights into a few days or a week, we have multiple weeks in one location to take it all in. We've also learned that many touristy things don't appeal to us, or that we've changed as people and now seek out good markets, restaurants, parks, and libraries instead of the top Google results for tourist attractions in each city.

Ani has spent more than half her life traveling this way and knows only this form of travel. I admire her for wanting to do one thing every day, then having plenty of downtime at our 'home' of the moment to focus on art, create, listen to audiobooks, and connect with friends online. However, sometimes I get frustrated and flip into the feeling that we must see or do several things in one day, and can't understand why she doesn't feel the same urge as I do. I get FOMO, and it is hard to shake.

Today, we got her to leave our hostel after some convincing, and Andy led us to a surprise lunch spot. It was a Mexican place near Ohori Park. We all smiled as we walked into the restaurant, happy to change our diet for a while to beans and rice with salsa and guacamole. Latin American music played, with Shakira singing, and a mix of Spanish, English, and Japanese came from the employees' mouths. There was a helpful sign at the table showing people how to eat a taco properly, with the head tilted at a 45-degree angle. Then I convinced Ani that I had a couple of surprises for her, and we unicycled to a nearby park with a large concrete dome and a slide. The last surprise was to take a paddle in the swan boats. It felt so good to finally do this touristy thing with her that I had been talking about all week. We stopped at our favorite coffee shop, Fika Coffee, on our way back and returned home feeling like we had taken in quite a few good sights today.

I share this because I sometimes envy people who have kids who love exploring and being outside all day. Ani doesn't. She knows herself, and I have to strike a balance between acceptance and pushing her to try new things and help her adjust to our new environment. Perhaps you have a child who also prefers to stay home. Hopefully, this makes you realize there are others in the world like your child.

(I read this aloud to Ani to make sure she was comfortable with me sharing this about her; she was).

Ani and one of her art pieces

On the swan paddle boat!

A Zen Tangle drawing by Irene

May 27th

Enjoyable food experiences this week –

In pursuit of warm meals, we go to restaurants. The microwave in our kitchenette makes great oatmeal, but it would be a stretch to make lunch in it, too. We take turns choosing our lunch spot every day. Ani started by winning the rock-paper-scissors game, so we went from youngest to oldest. One day this week, I took us to a recommended gyoza restaurant, only to find it had either moved or closed, replaced by a different Japanese restaurant. Then I searched for another gyoza restaurant. I led us to where I thought it would be, but realized Google Maps has its location in the middle of the street. That meant it was below street level. Japan, being an island nation, is creative in finding space, digging down, or going up to make room for businesses and lodging. We entered a beautiful underground shopping mall. The ceiling was made of iron shaped in flowers and geometric designs. There were restaurants, bakeries, a soy shop, a muffin store, business-clothing stores for salarymen, dress shops, cosmetic stores, drugstores, a sweet-potato store, and a soba restaurant we decided to eat at (somehow I still couldn't find the gyoza restaurant).

Ani chose a tempura restaurant. At first, I didn't want to go, as eating fried food in large quantities often gives me a headache the next day. Our rule is that we all go along, and if we don't like the food there, we can always eat later on our own. It was an enjoyable experience. We ordered from a vending machine, picked up our tickets, and waited inside the store for a seat at the tempura bar to open up. As people finished and left, those waiting in the queue would get up and move down the benches lining the wall. When we were seated, we were served pickled vegetables (lotus root, cabbage, and radish) with a spicy seaweed condiment, and we could help ourselves to unlimited tea and a darker barley tea. The meal came with rice, and I was pleased that the tempura eel I ordered was just the right amount and not overly oily.

On Sunday night, the udon noodle bar across the street was closed for the day, so I took us to a top-rated izakaya in our neighborhood.

The underground mall

Irene and Andy at the soba noodle restaurant

Tempura eel

They were full. We went to another one around the corner. They seated us, and just as we were getting settled, I noticed two people smoking at the table next to us. I almost stood to leave as the smoke hung in the air, but since we had come this far and felt as if the whole restaurant had already noticed us foreigners, we stuck it out. I used Google Translate to help me read the handwritten menus. There was a show on TV about Japanese people trying to build tiny hoop houses to grow rice. It seemed like a time competition they were participating in. I watched as they screwed on wiggle wire channels, and Andy commented on how they didn't even use GRK screws (the kind we had at the farm with star-shaped heads, which made using screws easier). It was a funny thing to think of our farming days in Hutchinson, MN, while seated in a smoke-filled Izakaya restaurant in Fukuoka, Japan. After our order of gyoza, udon soup, and salmon onigiri came, we paid and left. Ani was still hungry, so we stopped at 7-11, and she got herself some food before we came home.

Today I arranged a reservation at a vegan ramen restaurant. In Google Maps, the name says, "BUGORO ALL VEGAN (Only 3 seats)."

I asked ahead of time by email if I could order just noodles and broth for my daughter, but she said no; she would order one of the two set menu options. However, she offers a discount to people under 20. So, we made a reservation for all three seats and arrived at noon today. This restaurant has 5.0 stars on Google, based on over 50 reviews, which is rare. It is located in a residential neighborhood. I tried not to set my expectations too high, but upon arriving at the cozy home atmosphere, I was already impressed. The kitchen is right off the main dining room, and she quietly prepared the meals and brought them to us one by one.

Andy and his ramen soup

The main ramen soup was full of flavor and just the right amount of spice. Ani enjoyed it too, which made me feel great. She brought Ani her drink, made with butterfly pea flower, lemon juice, and simple syrup on the side. Ani enjoyed pouring the lemon juice into the pea-flower tea, watching it turn a violet hue. She didn't add the syrup. I ordered a matcha soy latte, and Andy had a probiotic soda that I believe contained cacao nectar and ginger. The dessert course was amazing. Ani had the lemon cake, Andy had a fruit parfait, and I had some matcha and chocolate ice cream. All came with smaller bite-sized desserts: a no-bake brownie bite, a matcha ball, a maple syrup panna cotta, and a pie-crust cookie. We brought some of the desserts home in a to-go container that I packed in my backpack. Some restaurants here in Japan don't allow you to take food to go, as they are very conscientious about food spoiling and causing illness. Today, I didn't ask, but I simply put the dessert items in my container while our host was in the kitchen. We left feeling very lucky to have experienced this meal together. I'm glad I reconsidered going to vegan restaurants with the family instead of solo.

 Ani with her dessert plate

May 28th

Sites of mutual fulfillment –

I follow Lucy AitkenRead on Instagram, and she posted about daily visiting a site of mutual fulfillment with your child some time ago. For her, it meant going to the playground, where she could sit back and watch her children play, while her kids loved running around and being physical. She suggested doing one activity or going to one place every day with your child that you both enjoy. Lately, Ani and I have been listening to audiobooks and doing art together in our hostel, and that has been a practice of mutual fulfillment. I have enjoyed looking at Brain Massage's Instagram page, copying some of their work, and adding my own touch. Ani has been making cute art books that she gifted to Andy and me. We have listened to The Giver by Lois Lowry (a few more challenging sections I listened to, then filled Ani in on what happened), Shiloh by Phyllis Reynolds Naylor, and are now on the second of this series, Shiloh Season.

If you have young kids at home, what do you do together that is mutually fulfilling?

Artwork by Ani. She gifted it to our favorite Udon noodle restaurant that was across from our hostel. They framed it and hung it up on the wall.

Zen tangle drawing and matcha latte with chocolate squares at our favorite cafe in Fukuoka

June 2nd
Our last days in Fukuoka, Japan –
We returned to the underground mall, realizing it was the
Tenchinka Museum of Art. It was built to resemble a European City
street, with wrought-iron ceilings.
https://www.tenchika.com/tenchikamuseum/

Ani and I visited the Asian Art Museum on the 7th floor of a local
mall.

We went to our favorite Udon Bar across from our hostel several
times. Ani gave them one of her drawings, and the next time we
went in, they had it framed and hung on the wall under the
television. We played many rounds of UNO there and learned
more about baseball, as they always had a game playing on the TV.

On our last full day there, we noticed a celebration underway. The
local theater, the Hakata Theater, was celebrating its 25th
anniversary. They held a boat parade, with several of the best
Kabuki actors and local officials seated in the boats as they
floated down the canal. So many people lined the streets and
threw confetti when they went past. It was unusual to see people
making a mess on purpose with confetti and hear some women
cry out in excitement as the Kabuki actors walked past (especially
the younger ones). It is usually quiet on the streets and in large
public spaces, so I smile to hear voices raised.

We visited TeamLab Forest's installation. This was whimsical and
fun, and we could go through the gym section as many times as
we wanted, as long as we kept moving forward. Four times was the
correct number of times for us. There was a room with big balls
floating mid-air that you could gently push around. The lights and
artistic displays made your brain question what was going on. In
the same complex was a Sanrio character shop, so Andy and Ani
went there as well. At the entrance, I sat with Ani's unicycle and
practiced Spanish using Duolingo.

Entering the Tenchinka Museum of Art/underground mall

Ani's drawing on display in the bottom right

SAKURAJIMA VOLCANIC ISLAND
June 3rd

We met with the Peterson Family yesterday to take public transportation and a ferry to Sakurajima Volcanic Island. On the short 15-minute ferry ride, there is a small udon noodle restaurant with good reviews, so we ate bowls of steaming hot udon noodles while on the deck of the ferry boat. The country of Japan sure knows how to make you feel cared for, with quick, delicious bowls of udon soup readily available all over. We watched Kagoshima grow smaller as we approached Sakurajima Island, home to the Showa Crater, which occasionally spits a puff of smoke from its volcanic activity.

There are many things to do on the island. Some weren't in season (the Mandarin oranges are ripe in December), and we missed the opportunity to dig into the sand and create our own hot foot baths as the tide came in and covered up the beach. So we started walking toward the foot bath, overlooking the volcano. Going on excursions with children is always interesting, as one never knows how far they will be willing to walk and what will excite them. We started walking again after soaking our feet in VERY hot water on a warm, sunny day (which made me feel even hotter). Most kids wanted to check out the public onsen (thermal-fed bathhouse). Since I don't have any tattoos, I am allowed to enter, so we decided to split up, and I went with Ani, Laila, and Silja to the onsen to bathe. It was the girls' first visit to a public bathhouse. We entered the women's side of the bathhouse and undressed. What at first felt a little strange for Ani quickly became normal as all of us were naked. A few older women were also in the bathhouse and were friendly toward us, trying to speak to us a bit as they bathed. I read that bathhouses are considered 'the great equalizer' here, where no one wears clothes; we are reminded that we are all the same beneath our garments. Since it was a hot day, I especially appreciated the cold bath, where we could cool off, then try the hot baths: one had thermal water, the hottest, and it was a bit murky from the minerals. The other hot bath was warm, with an area where electricity pulsed through the water. At first, it felt a little strange, but most of us tried it.

We didn't stare at the other women, but one can't help but notice their different shapes and sizes. The curved back of the elderly woman with a permanent hunch, the sagging skin of breasts and bellies. I have been feeling self-conscious lately, which I often do after we transition from one location to the next, partly because I know I have gained muscle from all the exercising I've been doing.

Silja and Ani

I'm sure I've gained a little weight from all the delicious foods we've been experiencing. It hit me there, sitting naked on a stool in the onsen, that I should love my body for its shape right now because I'm only going to get older. What a pity if I make it to the elderly woman's age and still wish my body looked a certain way. The older woman smiled at the splashing, joyous laughter of the cold plunge pool as the girls threw water at each other and themselves. I left feeling relaxed and somehow more connected to other women. Ani loved it and wanted to go with her friends again.

Sakurajima Volcanic Island

KAGOSHIMA, JAPAN

June 4th

Today, my good friend Ivana Petersen and I participated in a practice called "The Way of Tea." I had been calling it a tea ceremony, but our host gently corrected me, calling it "the way of tea." We arrived at the Birouen Tea Store in Kagoshima and were welcomed by an English translator and an intern who would be joining us for the ceremony. We walked to the second floor. After removing our shoes, we were introduced to three more people, one of them an older woman in a formal kimono, the master of the tea ceremony. She has been doing this practice for 30 years. We sat on tatami mats in the traditional tea room and met three others in formal kimonos. Eight people assisted with this ceremony for the three of us!

The calligraphic scroll on the wall read something like "mountain stream," meant to help one visualize being in nature. The tea master explained the fresh, natural flowers in a small hanging vase. I noticed a few leaves with holes from insects. They chose natural flowers you might find outside, not imported from a flower shop.

The tea master showed us how to eat sweets. It is traditional to eat something sugary before drinking matcha tea. Japanese sweets have been crafted with such care and precision that eating a sugary piece of art can feel special.

The ceremony itself was performed with great precision, slowly and methodically. I admired the woman who brought out the purified utensils in her formal kimono and watched her gracefully kneel and stand with great care, the kimono's wrapping limiting the range of motion in her legs. She prepared matcha tea for us, whisking the powdered green tea into a froth, then serving it to us one at a time. The tea master instructed us to rotate the bowls twice, then sip and enjoy; for the last sip, it was polite to make a slurping sound. It is hard for Westerners to make noise when drinking tea (and slurping noodles at restaurants) as we have been taught that it is impolite.

We had the chance to whisk matcha tea ourselves under the tea master's supervision. Then, they answered our questions. They also showed us a square tatami section on the floor and said they would lift it to place charcoal inside, heating the entire floor in winter.

I left the ceremony feeling lucky to have experienced it with my friend Ivana and to have been cared for by so many people. It reminded me of a meditative practice, as you are required to slow down, appreciate each movement, and sip with care.
I am still buzzing from the matcha; it is nearly midnight here. It is powerful!

Ivana and Irene whisking matcha

June 7th

We visited a public library in Kagoshima today. There was a significant section of English books in the children's area, and we spent about two hours reading books together. I know it is only a matter of time before Ani's interest in me reading to her will be gone, so I cherish this time with her. While we travel, we often seek out public libraries and always enjoy the quiet and the surrounding books.

Yesterday we took a trip on the Ferris wheel. It stands atop a mall surrounding Kagoshima Central Train Station. It was slow, yet it offered sweeping views of the city below. We hope to go again at night to see the difference. The kids wanted to explore the mall on their own, so we set up their devices to use the free Wi–Fi so they could get in touch with us if anything came up. We also gave them a set time to come and meet us at the entrance. They stayed together for 45 minutes and left before the set time.

**Ani, Silja, and Laila
near the ferris wheel**

Being in Japan at this time in Ani's life has been amazing regarding her learning independence. It is common for children as young as 5 to be out in public, walking home from school or walking to different destinations alone. The vehicles stop so well for pedestrians, and hardly anyone jaywalks, so traffic isn't a concern. The other day in Fukuoka, we were waiting to cross a side street to reach a park. The lights went through one cycle, and the green walk signal never appeared.

Then we realized we had to push the button for this crosswalk. We pressed it, and the man across the street (only 12 feet away) pressed the button too, and we both waited patiently for the traffic lights to cycle again and let us cross. Mind you, there were no vehicles at the intersection. Everyone just waits for their turn to maintain the order of things. Ani has been enjoying visiting local grocery stores and convenience stores on her own to buy the food she likes.

I will miss the walkability and sense of safety when we return to the States.

Irene hugging the English children's book section

June 10th

On Saturday, Ani had an 'independent day' from us. That meant she packed her bag and rode her unicycle to the Petersons' home (about 1 mile away). She stopped on the way to get breakfast from a convenience store and messaged us when she arrived. Andy and I took the day to ourselves: we ran together in the morning, then went out for lunch at a vegan South Indian restaurant, and came home to do computer work in the afternoon.

Today, we met up with the Petersons for lunch at a pizza restaurant that served pocket pizzas. Then Ivana and I walked to Sengan-en, a traditional Japanese garden and former residence of a feudal lord. While in the garden, we visited a cat shrine, the burial ground for two of the seven cats that went with an expeditionary army to Korea with Yoshihiro. Yohihiro used the cats' eyes to tell the time of day. "Round at six, like an egg at eight and four, like a persimmon seed at ten and two, and a needle at midday."

It was a long walk; when I got home, I had covered over 9 miles. Our conversations about parenting, travel, and unschooling filled me up.

Playing in a fountain at a favorite park in Kagoshima

Ani and Irene unicycling

June 11th

Our friend Tommy rented a car today that was big enough to fit all eight of us inside. We drove an hour south to Ibusuki to visit the Saraku Sand Bath Hall. This part of Japan has many thermal pools. You can take a sand bath at this place, meaning you dress in a yukata (a bathing robe), then walk outside to the beach where attendants dig a long hole in the sand to lie in. Then they cover you with hot sand, and you rest for 10 minutes, feeling its weight on your body. No photographs are allowed in the sand bathing hall, so if you'd like to see what it looks like, you'll have to search online. Then we rinsed off and entered a mixed–gender onsen. This one allowed tattoos so that Andy could enjoy the onsen (thermal bathing room). There was a large hot thermal pool, a smaller cold pool, and a sauna.

We visited the Tosenkyo Flowing "Somen" Noodle restaurant for lunch. This place is beside many streams, with carp swimming in the water. The noodles you order arrive, and you dip them in cold water that swirls around in a whirlpool. Then, you dip them into the sauce and eat them. I had been wanting to do this all week, so having the opportunity to share it with friends was delightful.

Then we visited a local playground. We searched the grass for living things and found many insects and a lizard. Anton caught the lizard, and we even removed a tick from it with tweezers.

We adjusted as the day progressed, trying to meet everyone's needs in the car. I write this because it is natural to post only positive things online, but in reality, some kids want to go home, misunderstandings happen, and minor accidents occur on playgrounds. I'm grateful for understanding, caring parents and friends.

The flowing noodle restaurant

Walking into the Saraku Sand Bath Hall

June 14th

Today, we visited a bear-themed shabu-shabu restaurant for lunch. The bears are made of gelatin and so detailed that they're incredible. Heat them on a gas stove in front of you. When the shoulders are submerged, add the broth enhancer and seasonings, then cook the vegetables and meat slices one at a time. At the end, you add noodles or dumplings to cook in the flavored broth. It was delightful. Andy and Ani went last week with the Petersons, but I missed it because I had a scheduled phone call at the same time. This time, we could go as a family; they knew exactly which sauces to choose from and how it all worked. I felt fortunate to have had the experience.

We packed our checked luggage and brought three bags to the local convenience store to have them shipped to Ishigaki, our next destination. Each piece costs around $20 to send. When we take the train and plane tomorrow, we will only have our carry-on backpack and a few changes of clothes. The domestic luggage service here in Japan has been excellent. I am especially grateful for it as I have a slight injury in my right forearm. It started when I tried to lift weights that were too heavy in a Thai gym. It heals, then I accidentally re-injure it, so now I'm paying close attention to how I use my arm and trying hard not to lift heavy things with it or strain it. I recently re-injured it by pulling myself up a rope feature at a playground. I want it to heal up completely! With our travel lifestyle, having functioning body parts is necessary.

We bid farewell to our friends, the Petersons, yesterday afternoon. We really enjoyed spending almost two weeks with them here in Kagoshima, and we are making plans to meet up with them again next year.

I have been enjoying training for my upcoming races. There is a river here that I've been running along. The stepping stones are fun to cross over. When we move to Ishigaki tomorrow, I hope to start open-water swimming practice on a beach there. Apparently, there are beaches where they net off the swimming area to keep jellyfish out and prevent stings.

Fingers crossed, my arm cooperates, and I don't find a jellyfish that snuck through the netting. It is forecast to be tropical, with high temperatures and humidity, so a swim will be welcome.

Gelatin bear that turned into broth

Stepping stones over river

Shipping our luggage at 7–11

ISHIGAKI, JAPAN

June 16th
On our flight to Ishigaki Island yesterday, I watched The Social
Dilemma on Netflix. It is a powerful movie that explains several
problems with social media.

*The Mental Health Dilemma: A 5,000-person study found that
higher social media use correlated with self-reported mental and
physical health and life satisfaction declines.
American Journal of Epidemiology, 2017

*The Democracy Dilemma: The # of countries with political
disinformation campaigns on social media doubled in the past two
years.
The New York Times, 2019

*The Discrimination Dilemma: 64% of the people who joined
extremist groups on Facebook did so because the algorithms
steered them there.
Internal Facebook report, 2018

I visited their website and followed the social media reboot, in
which I pledged to do the following for the next 7 days:
*Create a scroll-free space in my life
I won't use my mobile device 30 minutes before bed or 30
minutes after waking up.
*Reclaim my screen time for connection
I will turn off unnecessary notifications or disable them on apps
that use surveillance-based algorithms to decide what information
I see.
*Free myself of the manipulation engines
I will disable autoplay features where possible and never watch a
recommended video to avoid rabbit holes.
*Take care before I share
To combat social media's propensity to spread misinformation
and play into my biases, I will pause before sharing content to
check the source and question my motives for posting.

There is a guide to talking with children about social media that I plan to review with Ani.

I recommend watching this movie, checking out the website (https://www.thesocialdilemma.com/), disabling video autoplay on Facebook and YouTube, and turning off notifications from these apps on your phone.

Outside the Ishigaki Airport upon our arrival. Our Airbnb hosts took our photo.

June 17th

We arrived via plane on Ishigaki Island on Saturday. Our apartment host, Risa, her sister, and her mother met us at the airport to welcome us. They speak little English, but are comfortable with Google Translate. Using the Translate app, they asked what we wanted to do that day, and I said we wanted to go grocery shopping. On the way back, they brought us to a large grocery store, gave us reusable bags to carry our groceries, and waited for us. Then they stopped at a confectionery shop, and we picked up several treats (a baked matcha donut, a chocolate donut, and banana bread). Risa insisted on buying these items for us. Then they brought us to our home. We are staying in their childhood home, with the mother and father who live in their own home below us.

The next day, Risa asked whether we wanted to do anything with her on the island. I mentioned that I wanted to find a place to swim, as I'm training for a triathlon. We met, and she called the fitness club to ask if we could swim there once we were in the club's parking lot. They said yes, so she drove the route again so I would know how to walk to the club on my own (it is a 10-minute walk). Then we went inside, and once we discussed the cost and the time it was available, the club employee suggested we go to a nearby beach to swim that day, since it is free and she enjoys training there. Since Risa and her sister were off work, they agreed to take us there so we could swim at the beach. Later in the week, when they had to work, I could go to the fitness club to swim on my own. Granted, this was all communicated in Japanese through the translator, so it took patience and understanding to convey the ideas. In that instant, Ani was bummed, as she doesn't love beaches, and saw the beautiful, clean pool through the glass. She agreed to go, and once we arrived, we were pleasantly surprised to find the fabulous beach. The swimming area was netted off to keep out the jellyfish, and the water was warm. I swam for 20+ minutes and happily discovered my arm didn't hurt. They had showers to rinse off the salt water.

Our host's sister was kind enough to pick Ani up, bring her to the foot bath to rinse the sand from her feet, then carry her back to sit and put on her shoes. The Japanese people are so kind and generous with their actions and time. May I remember their generosity and share it with others in the future!

Our host's mom loves plants and has a beautiful potted garden along her street. A plant growing in the parking area has attracted Paper Kite Butterflies to lay eggs. Their cocoons are shiny and gold, and discovering them makes you feel delighted and in awe of Mother Nature. There are at least 20 of them on this plant. We are enjoying watching their life cycle. When I returned from a run, I saw two young recently emerged butterflies resting with their wings outstretched this morning.

Paper Kite Butterfly cocoons

A new Paper Kite Butterfly

June 20th

We have been taking things slow this week. The heat and humidity here are extreme. Our phones always show an "Excessive Heat Warning" on the homescreen, with highs around 91 degrees F (32 C) and 82% humidity (Dew point at 82 degrees F or 27 C). We learned a good lesson about checking the temperature of a location before traveling there. I thought we had learned this lesson with Thailand, but we failed to research the island's highlights at this time of year before booking our trip. What is nice about our time here is our beautiful apartment with lovely hosts. Our own kitchen, washing machine, access to a grocery store, a fitness club down the way, and a bicycle. We haven't eaten out yet, but we are making our meals at home. Sometimes I bring in pre-made food from the grocery store and heat it (last night we had delicious gyoza that were pre-made, but I pan-fried them to heat them and make the bottom nice and crisp, alongside miso soup with a miso bonito paste that simply needed hot water to become delicious soup, and edamame).

Ani has a stomach bug. She asked me, "Mom, why is there sickness? What is the point of it?" I had to reflect on this, but eventually said something like: It is part of being human that, when we are sick, the body is out of balance and has a chance to reset itself to become healthy again. It also helps us cultivate patience as we wait for our bodies to heal. We recently listened to The Giver aloud. This book is about a world where most humans no longer have feelings or memories, except for The Giver, who holds everyone's memories and is training a 12-year-old boy to take his place. So I also brought that up in the conversation, reminding her that life has its highs and lows. If it were all the same, it wouldn't be exciting.

I still can't wait for her to be fully healed so we can explore and see a few more things on this island. I am being patient!

I swam at the local athletic club on Monday afternoon. I haven't had much experience swimming, but went for a workout using Ani's goggles (which cover the eyes and nose).

It was helpful to have them, but blowing air out of my nose felt a bit awkward, as the whole goggle kept slipping off my face. I will purchase goggles for myself today and a swim cap to wear for future training sessions. After 35 minutes in the pool and the heat, I came home and took a 45-minute nap.

I look forward to improving my swimming, but it takes a lot of energy from me in this early phase. Yesterday morning, I set out for a 6-mile run, leaving around 8 a.m. to beat the heat, but after 2 miles, with my shirt nearly soaked in sweat, I turned around and walked home. I'll try again later today, closer to sunset, to get in a run.

Sunset over the rice fields

On a run

122

June 22nd

I was reminded of how important human interaction is today. Ani had been going through a tough time these past few days; it was a combination of tummy bug, homesickness, and loneliness. We arranged to meet with our host, Risa, and her sister this afternoon to see a few spots on the island. When they arrived, I was surprised to see they also had two young children with them, Risa's grandchildren, aged 7 and 9. At first, Ani was a bit shy, but after we spent some time driving, the children used Google Translate to communicate and laughed and played together like children. We stopped at a garden full of Shisa figurines in the backyard of a pottery shop. We passed Arakawa Falls, and Andy and I hopped out to look at the falls. When we saw a freshwater swimming hole with cool water, we returned to take the children for a swim. Swimming and cooling off our bodies from the high heat and humidity was delightful. Then we stopped at Kabira Bay, Ishigaki's number one tourist destination. It has beautiful blue waters, a soft sand beach, and gorgeous views.

I am thankful for Google Translate. It also allowed us to attend a glassmaking workshop yesterday, where the expert instructor guided us through making our own galaxy necklaces made out of glass. Using the translate app, we learned a bit more about each other. She went to Seattle to study glass blowing. I shared that I studied at the University of Washington.

Shishas

She said her English isn't very strong, and when she was in Seattle, Translate didn't exist. She said that the other students were very nice. I can understand how challenging it is to fit into another culture without knowing the language. Here in Japan, I am grateful for how kind people are to foreigners. I don't think I can say the same for some people in the United States who interact with foreigners, which makes me feel ashamed, and makes me want humans to do better in this, no matter their country.

I realize I am sharing the highlights of what we have done over the past few days. Other things that happened include Ani and me watching The Wizard of Oz (we recently finished reading the book together), watching the movie Leo, reading books together while doing watercoloring, listening to Circle Round, cooking, some homeschooling, and resting so Ani could fully recover from her stomach bug.

Our glass blown necklaces

Shisha statue

June 26th

We spent our last full day on Ishigaki Island taking public transportation to Arakawa Falls for a picnic lunch and swim. The fresh water is cold, and the sound of the falls makes you feel as if you are in a sound bath, refreshing your spirit and body.

We have learned much from living in this hot, humid climate over the past 10 days. I decided to pay admission to the fitness club to use their treadmill, something I would usually never do. Every new thing that I do takes some courage. I have to be comfortable asking for what I want, using Google Translate to help me. It is easy to take for granted living in a country where your native tongue is spoken. On the treadmill, I could listen to a few podcasts (Wait Wait... Don't Tell Me! and The Moth Radio Hour) while focusing on the outside foliage and patiently watching the miles go by. I did my long run for the week - 7 miles. I couldn't have managed it outside with the severe heat warning.

Ani and I swam at the fitness club earlier in the week. It was refreshing and lifted our spirits.
We will start our journey to the States tomorrow with a flight to Okinawa, a one-night stay, and then a long flight to Minnesota. Ani is pleased to be going back to family and friends. There have been some challenging moments this past week as we waited for our departure day to arrive.

Cooling off near the waterfall

June 28th
Farewell Japan
I asked our host, Risa, to arrange a taxi to the Ishigaki Airport, since I know she works during the week. She surprised me the night before our departure by saying she would pick us up and drop us off during her lunch break, as she would like to see us off.

She gave Ani a blue t-shirt with a manta ray on the front, having overheard Ani tell her grandchildren that her favorite color was blue the previous weekend.

On our way to the airport, we chatted (using Google Translate) about the weather, and Risa said she was glad it had been calm. There haven't been any typhoons yet. I didn't realize that was possible, and I was grateful for this perspective. I also learned that there are seven (not six) types of pineapple on Ishigaki, and there are only two months of the year to enjoy them fresh. We were lucky to experience this pineapple season.

While waiting to board our flight, they offered pre-boarding to adults with young children, and all at once I remembered the many flights we had taken advantage of this on, and realized that Ani is no longer a young child. It is bittersweet to see her mature and grow, yet I feel my parenting journey is already halfway through.

Once settled in our Okinawa Airbnb, Andy checked our flights for today. He received an email from Japan Airlines two days ago, canceling the first flight from Okinawa to Tokyo. After chatting via text and calling the airline, he sorted it out and had us rebooked. There was some confusion around his SkyMiles number being filled out with 'Andy' instead of his full name, 'Andrew.' So the system canceled that flight. I am in awe of how many things can happen when traveling, and I'm glad Andy knows to check and call to sort them out. While he waited on hold, I went out to explore and found one geocache, so I can claim Japan as a new country in my 'finds.' I also walked the main shopping street and took in the vibe of Okinawa.

Andy with our luggage at the Okinawa Airport

The Okinawa Airport had so many beautiful orchids!

This morning, while waiting for the Monorail from our Airbnb to the Airport, we had to wait for another train to come because the first was so full you couldn't fit another person on. We squeezed into the next one, me holding my backpack above Andy's head to give our bodies more space. Thankfully, it was a short stop until more people got off, and as the train went on, more space opened up. Our mood is lighthearted and happy as we navigate back to Minnesota. There are so many things I will miss about Japan. It has been good to us, and we would love to come again.

MINNESOTA

July 1st

One of the things I love about returning to Minnesota after living abroad for a long time is the change in perspective that comes from being immersed in different cultures. Some call it reverse culture shock. I like to think of it as cultural awareness. After being in places where we knew no one, returning to Minnesota, and building all the connections and relationships we've cultivated, I feel like I've won a social connection jackpot.

My father picked us up from the airport, and it felt so good to have him there, waiting for us. I know he prefers to park in short-term parking and walk in to greet us, not just wait for us to come outside to the curb. I know he will always be there 30-60 minutes early, despite us trying to time it just right. We will drive back to his home through side streets, taking in the neighborhoods instead of rushing on the freeway. My mother prepared a meal for us at 3 pm, an early dinner of chicken, asparagus, cornbread, and an apple crisp. For her, this is a big act of love, since she usually prepares food with my dad, which takes a lot of energy. My dad helped peel and chop the apples and was surprised when she finished it solo, baking it and having it ready for our dessert.
On the first night home, all my energy went to eating, showering, and then crashing into bed (our own bed and pillows!) and sleeping by 6 pm. My usual routine of helping put Ani to sleep didn't happen, as my dad filled in for me so I could sleep. What a gift.

Thanks to jet lag, we've been waking up early. Yesterday, we were all awake by 3 am Central Time (5 pm Japan Time). I enjoy listening to the birdsong that starts around 5 am, which I know so well but haven't heard in so long, it sounds new. I remember those bird songs. They differ from those in Southeast Asia.
The weather here is comfortable. Highs in the 70s with low humidity make it easy to run. Andy has been joining me in the mornings, as Ani feels safe being left at home with my parents.

People greet you in English when you pass them. In Japan, people don't stare and generally don't acknowledge you in the street when passing.

I attended a Genelin family reunion with my mom and dad yesterday in southern Minnesota. I don't know many relatives on that side of the family, but it was fun to meet a few new people and enjoy a traditional potluck meal. I admired all the noodle salads, potato salads (at least one from a grandmother's recipe), and at least eight crockpots full of meat with beans, sauce, or sauerkraut. It was such a good representative of a midwestern potluck and so different from the food we had been eating in Japan, which featured rice, noodles, kelp, seaweed, fish, egg rolls, sushi, bamboo, lotus root, carrot, tofu, and tempura.

Irene, Kay, and Mike at the family reunion

Irene and Kay

July 7th

We are almost over jet lag, and enjoying the connections we have here in Minnesota. It is nice to have neighbor kids who stop by, people who invite us to dinner and a bonfire, and a nice kitchen to host others for meals. I've been training for my upcoming triathlon and marathon. People actually say hello to you as they pass, unlike the quiet, polite Japanese custom of not making eye contact and walking ahead. One person commented positively on my swimming, and another person guessed my age to be 55 (after I realized he wasn't quite in his correct state of mind, there was no way I was going to tell him my age when he asked me. I had him guess). I tried not to take anything personally, but kept checking off my training sessions. Today, I went for my long run of the week: 8 miles. I ran through Long Lake Park, saw a deer, ate a few wild mulberries, and spotted black cap raspberries. I listened to Wait Wait Don't Tell Me and the Moth Story Hour. The Moth podcast was so funny that I was belly-laughing and crying tears of joy. That was a fun way to complete a long run.
I unicycled to the Mill City Farmers Market and ran into several friends we knew from the farming world who were selling their produce there. It is such a bustling, fun market; I always enjoy my time there. I recommend the chai and momos! The Stone Arch Bridge is currently closed for maintenance, so I took the newly renovated Central Ave Bridge and admired the bike lanes.

We purchased a tandem bicycle second-hand last night. I found it on Facebook Marketplace. It is a nice tandem, with an Osells sticker. Terry Osell once owned and ran a bicycle shop in St. Anthony, MN, that sold bicycles, tandems, and unicycles! That was where I purchased my first unicycle and had my custom artistic uni made by his employee, Paul. Andy and Ani took their first ride on it today, and we hope to cruise the streets of the Twin Cities on the cycle while we are here. I also appreciate that we are keeping the correct one-wheel-to-one-rider ratio, which is essential in the unicycling community.

My favorite meals this week (for inspiration, for those of you reading): make your own burritos; roast chicken and potatoes; shepherd's pie; zucchini soup; lemon-raspberry bars; chocolate-avocado tarts; and flank steak with potatoes and slaw.

Our new tandem bicycle

Momos from the Mill City Market

BEMIDJI, MINNESOTA

July 18th

UNICON 21, the International Unicycling Championships and Convention, is underway in Bemidji, MN.

I have enjoyed watching the artistic freestyle routines. Sometimes I get tears in my eyes watching the performers. I can feel their dedication, desire, and love for unicycling, and I remember the thrill of performing out there.

I participated in the 10km race yesterday. I took 2nd place in my 30+ age group and 11th overall among women.
Today, I participated in the Muni Cross Country race on Giants Ridge in Biwabik, MN. Waking at 5 a.m. for the bus ride was rough, but these conventions are all about fitting in as many events and activities as possible in a few weeks.

It is interesting to return to UNICON and see what roles I take on. For example, today, there was one younger girl in my MUni heat who was off her uni on the side of the trail about three miles into the race. I stopped to check on her, the momma bear in me coming out. Thankfully, a bicycle support team not far behind took over, so I could keep riding.

I tried to offer words of encouragement to a very nervous friend before her freestyle routine. I reflected on how much meditation and breathwork have helped me in my life. I wish I had known about these tools when I was younger and competing in artistic routines!

I continue to work on ego management. I want to remain the fastest unicyclist without proper race training, yet recognize that younger riders want the medals more and should have their chance to win them. Now I see the parents supporting the younger riders, and I'm trying to act like a fast parent who still loves unicycling.

Irene during the 10km race

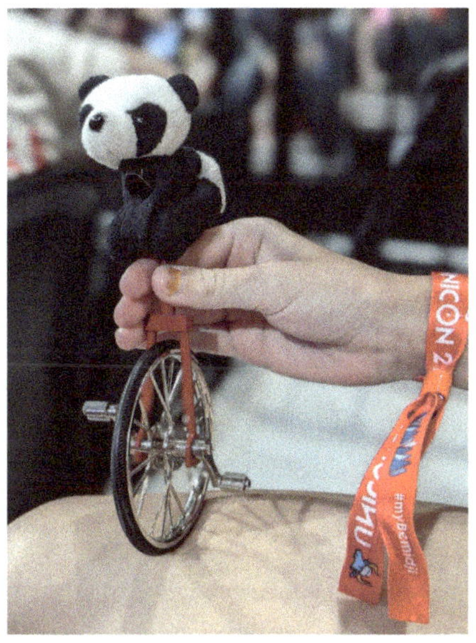

BB with her unicycle at the opening ceremonies

Lena and Brandi

Andy and Ani volunteering at the Trials Competition

July 23rd

This week has been full of connections, races, and awe. There has also been a bit of overwhelm, crying, and sadness. I can summarize it by saying it has been regular life during UNICON (the International Unicycling Competition and Championships).

We connected with our hosts, Andy, Brandi, and Lena Larkin, this weekend, as they were all home, and welcomed three friends from Connecticut. Another 9-year-old girl, Elsie, stayed with us at the Larkins, which made it fun for Ani, Lena, and Elsie. We played on the Lake and the Mississippi, the girls filmed a dance together, we visited the Art Festival in town, had a bonfire, and shared several meals.

UNICON races are happening every day. On Sunday morning, Andy organized a fun triathlon. We swam in Lake Bemidji, rode a unicycle about 5 km, and ran 2.2 miles to the Paul Bunyan Statue and back. I took 5th place for the women.

I raced in a long double-loop of Lake Bemidji yesterday. I took 9th place overall among females and 4th in the 30+ category. The highlight of the race was chatting with a strong unicyclist named Sofia, 13, from Holland, for probably 10 miles. Her parents were excellent at cheering her on (and me, since we rode at a similar pace). It was also a beautiful course, with a view of the vast Lake Bemidji on the right for nearly 3 hours. The course was 33.5 miles long, and I was ready to get off because of saddle soreness by the end.

We watched many fantastic artistic unicycle routines. One of my favorite group routines was from Japan; they called their group Infinity. They took first place with a flawless routine. I had tears of joy in my eyes when they finished, moved by the depth of their expertise and performance. They received a standing ovation. There was also a family from Pennsylvania who performed a small-group routine with two parents and a 6-year-old girl (and her younger brother made an appearance). That also made me tear up at the beauty of their bravery in stepping onto the floor and performing for a huge crowd.

QR Code for Pairs Freestyle Routine

Irene getting wet during cyclocross

Andy putting the paddleboard in the water 3 miles away from our lodging

The young girl had just learned to ride three months earlier, and it was a sweet routine. TCUC (The Twin Cities Unicycle Club) performed with 38 riders, and I could tell they were having a blast in their brightly colored costumes and to the music of The Minions. I have so much respect for all the riders and the people coordinating the routines, knowing how long it takes to assemble something like this.

July 25th
UNICON (the International Unicycling Competition and Convention) continues in Bemidji, MN. Scan the QR Code to see the inspirational video of the Pairs Expert Freestyle World Champions from Japan: ANZU Hashimoto and Mayuko Kogi.

I raced cyclocross yesterday. It is a fun race with people handing out snacks and getting riders wet with squirt guns and bubbles along the course. Several people dressed up in fun costumes as well. I enjoyed the race and believe I was the only mother to finish the Elite female race, placing 11th out of 32 women in that category.

135

We watched the Expert Trials competitors last night at the Sanford Arena, and man, it was inspiring to see them pull off amazing lines. There was one with a slack line where the female riders had to go halfway out, then gap to a pallet. The men had to ride halfway out on the slack line, then turn 90 degrees while jumping to a very narrow skinny (the 1" side of a 1" x 4" piece of wood), continue riding about 15', and end by touching a pallet, then the ground. I was so inspired that I tried balancing my uni on the slackline at the back of our friend's home today. It will take some practice to feel comfortable letting go of a hand and mastering this skill.

Andy put Brandi's Stand Up Paddleboard (SUP) in the back of our car this morning, and I dropped him off at a bridge across the Mississippi River about 3 miles away. He paddled home (against a wind, but with the current), which took him just over an hour. He enjoys paddleboarding. I enjoy watching him learn a new sport and share his knowledge with me and the others who see him paddle. When we were in Thailand this past year, he bought an inflatable SUP and paddled it out on the ocean every day. He gave rides to other members of the Traveling Village and let others borrow the paddleboard. Our friends from Italy recently shared that they followed his lead and purchased a SUP as well.

One of my low points was realizing that I have such a passion for unicycling and could watch all the events at UNICON and participate in even more, but I am in a family time of life and have to consider everyone's needs. Perhaps Ani will grow into this passion, perhaps not. I hope she discovers something and is as passionate about it as I am about unicycling. Andy and Ani volunteered to judge a trial line yesterday, and today we decorated some of the trial lines with our artistic talents. Andy and Ani met Walker, the artist behind the fun design for the UNICON logos. He has been a kind ally in our conversations about art with Ani.

July 29th
Connections

When we travel slowly through different countries, there are times when the only person we know is our Airbnb host, because we ask them to meet up for dinner or a drink. The abundance of connections I've felt over the past few weeks at UNICON has been a stark contrast. What is neat about UNICON is that you can meet international friends every two years in different parts of the world and make new connections. I think about relationships and how it takes time to cultivate them. One of the nice things about being in MN is stepping back into the accessibility of friends and family and spending time together. Andy's cousin had a 60th-birthday party, and we stopped by on our way back from Bemidji. We were free, and it was on our way, so we stopped to say hello.

The last unicycle race I participated in was the criterium. It was a short course in a parking lot with many 180-degree turns. It tested your ability to maintain speed as you curved and turned sharply around corners. There were two waves of 10 women in the unlimited category. The top 5 finishers from each heat (4 laps) did one more final race (6 laps). I participated in the final heat and finished 7th. I was smiling most of the race, as it was so much fun to be out there riding and hearing cheers from the crowd. I even cheered for the women around me, and when one of them overtook me, I encouraged her. Overall, I have found a good sense of sportsmanship in unicycling.

 Family photo near Paul and Babe

Irene trying the slack line with a hand from Andy

Irene during the criterium

HUTCHINSON, MINNESOTA
August 4th
This week, we returned from Bemidji and had a few days to unpack
and settle in. Then we went to Hutchinson to visit Joan Cotter and
a few friends, and to get our teeth cleaned.

My friend Martin developed a weight-training program called Papa
Power Hour. He created this business while traveling with the
Traveling Village in Southeast Asia. It is a truly great program that
takes only 15-30 minutes a few times a week to help you build
strength and stay mobile as you raise children and move through
life. He is coaching me in preparation for my upcoming Triathlon. I
enjoyed a 5-day deload phase after UNICON, and now I am
starting an intense training block leading up to the September 8th
triathlon and October 6th marathon. This morning I went for a 10-
mile run to the Mill City Farmers Market, and my dad picked me
up.

We are painting some of the basement walls, and Ani plans to
create a play area down there for her toys and stuffed animals. It
is in the same place where my brother used to run a radio station,
where he was a DJ using tapes. He even let me play DJ for a while,
and although the broadcast didn't reach very far, our neighbor Bob
said he could hear us, so that was something our younger selves
could be proud of. It makes me smile to know the same spot is
being used for fun again. Ani learned a lot about properly
preparing a wall using spackling, a putty knife, and sandpaper.

Preparing the basement wall

**Visiting Layla, our former dog
who now lives on a friend's farm**

NEW BRIGHTON, MINNESOTA

August 7th

This week, we checked out the Herbivorous Butcher in NE Minneapolis and tried a couple of their fake cheezes. I unicycled along the Mississippi, then turned around, met Andy and Ani at the Herbivorous Butcher, and rode back to New Brighton together. Then I went for a four-mile run, which felt tough after 20 miles on the bike. This is the start of an intense month of training for my upcoming triathlon. Today, I took a short nap because my body needed extra recovery.

Painting bamboo on the basement walls

Yesterday, I dropped Andy off in Big Lake to bicycle 40 miles with our Austrian unicycle friend, Felix.

We continue working on making a special area in the basement. Now, one wall is draped with beautiful bamboo stalks. Our neighbors were kind enough to lend us their projector to get started. We outlined the wall using chalk, a trick we learned from our graffiti experience in Da Nang, Vietnam.

August 16th

On Tuesday, we ate at Owamni by the Sioux Chef (owamni.com). The restaurant uses no colonized ingredients, such as dairy, wheat, or refined sugar. It is located next to the Mississippi River in downtown Minneapolis. We met there with our former fruit mentor, Carmen Converse, to chat and catch up, as we hadn't seen each other in four years. I recommend visiting the restaurant. A few of our dishes were spicy, but you can ask the waitstaff for recommendations.

I have continued training for my triathlon by swimming, running, and unicycling. This week, I am scaling back my running to give my knees a much-needed rest, as they were sore after a long 14-mile training run last Saturday. I had an acupuncture session today with Dr. Wei Liu, and he placed many needles around my knees to stimulate energy flow and support healing.

I visited the Shoreview Community Center swimming pool on Tuesday morning to swim laps and marveled at the remodel since I last visited as a child. I didn't love swimming before this year, but now that I have defined workouts, a swim cap, and nice goggles, I'm starting to enjoy the feeling of swimming and how it works the whole body.

We unicycled the New Brighton Parade last Saturday morning. It is a special parade for me, as seeing the Twin Cities Unicycle Club in it 27 years ago sparked my desire to learn to unicycle. The weather was cool and sunny, the club had a big turnout, and it felt like a vibrant unicycle show with an appreciative crowd.

I continue to listen to Marshall Rosenberg's podcast on Nonviolent Communication – "Marshall Rosenberg NVC Training by Joe Public." I'm on session #6 of 9 and am learning many takeaways on how to listen empathetically, guess what another person needs, and state my observations, needs, and requests. I believe it will take months of practice to become proficient at this, but it is a communication method that connects and nourishes. Empathy is listening to someone and being with them in their time of trouble. Sympathy is when you shift the focus from them to yourself, having gone through something similar. Many people (myself included) struggle to stay empathetic without trying to sympathize or offer advice.

Marshall gave an example of a friend who would recount her day's activities to him at length. After some time, Marshall asked her, "Why are you telling me what happened at work today?" She said, "Because I thought it was important to say." Then Marshall said, "What response would you like from me after you tell me these things?" She thought for a while and said, "I don't need a response, I just need to say it." He said, "Oh, well, do you mind if I read a book while you talk to me?" She said, "You better not!" He was joking, but wanted to convey that she didn't need to speak uselessly. Later, she told him she noticed others didn't always like talking to her, and that the interaction helped her think through what she would say before she spoke.

Delicious foods created in our kitchen this week include: veggie chicken soup, toasted pecans, apple-peach pies, bread, roast chicken, riced cauliflower with chicken-pepper gravy, boiled beets, sweet corn, several meals of fried rice with local veggies, zucchini muffins, waffles, and oatmeal.

John on a group ride in Stillwater with me and several other unicyclists

August 19th

Ani attended summer camp at the Bell Museum of Natural History this past week. She said she was glad she participated and would do it again next year. The museum is well-organized, and the educational program is thoughtfully designed.

I organized a long-distance unicycle ride in Stillwater last Saturday with seven other cyclists. We met at Square Lake and rode the 18-mile cycling leg of the triathlon route I will be doing on September 8th. It was overcast and misty, which reminded me of all the long-distance rides I organized while living in Seattle, where it was more often than not raining. I have good memories of getting together with others to ride long-distance unicycles, and last Saturday, I added another memory to that part of my brain.

I finished listening to Marshall Rosenberg's podcast series on Nonviolent Communication - "Marshall Rosenberg NVC Training by Joe Public." There is much I could write about that moved me. Today, I will share from episode #9, The Role of Sincere Gratitude. Marshall speaks about the difference between praise and compliments, and between sincere gratitude and mere thanks. He frames sincere gratitude to someone as follows: explain what actions that person has taken, tell them how it has made you feel, what need it has fulfilled for you, and how it has added to your life. It isn't always easy for others to receive gratitude.

After listening to this series, I realize how often I give praise and compliments. I'm trying to think of other ways to say thank you so the person realizes which actions I am thankful for and why.

August 29th

Wisdom with aging?

In 2007, I ran my first marathon while recovering from bronchitis. The night before racing, I had difficulty sleeping because of my cough. I remember taking cough syrup that had codeine in it to help me sleep. I ran the race, coughing, and finished the last few miles by walking. I thought, "Yes! I did it!" I can honestly say I have completed a marathon. I cringe when I remember this story and how much I pushed through to complete this goal.

This year, when deciding how to celebrate my 40th birthday, I signed up for a Sprint Triathlon on my birthday date and the Twin Cities Marathon, which would be one month later. I am passionate about my training, as I feel so good from the endorphins it releases. I feel like I am getting stronger. I am also navigating a knee injury because it turns out my knees get sore after long runs (12 miles+). I spoke with my trainer and have decided to take a break from running again this week, focusing on swimming and unicycling, with daily videos to strengthen the knee and loosen my hips. I don't know if I can run in the marathon. I am sad about a potential goal that won't be achieved. I wonder if there is wisdom that comes with aging, because I don't want to hurt my body and risk a longer-term knee injury just to say I accomplished something. I have already done that.

Downtown Minneapolis while on an evening unicycle ride

Our travels have also helped me better understand the culture I grew up in. In America, there is an emphasis on individual gain and strength, pushing through meal times to get more work done, sacrificing health to earn more, and pursuing titles to add to one's resume.

I am sharing this because my need to follow my word is strong, and I feel like I'm disappointing someone (who? myself?) if I don't complete what I say I will. I'm learning it's okay to shift with life, with how my body feels, and with my family's needs. Can you think of a time when you set out to do something, tuned into your inner wisdom, stopped, and changed course?

Andy and Ani after an amazing thunderstorm

September 3rd

FORTY!

Thank you to all who wrote to me wishing me a happy birthday. I spent the day with my family, unicycling, visiting the Walker Art Sculpture Garden, and eating delicious food.

I received a Romanian text from a dentist I had visited, wishing me a happy birthday. I smiled, realizing that even in Romania, they message their clients.

Family photo at the Walker Sculpture Garden

The Cherry on the Spoon in the Walker Sculpture Garden

Family photo at the Walker Sculpture Garden using a see through mirror

Family photo with my brother, Matt, Kay, and Mike

September 6th

We took a road trip south to Iowa. Along the way, we stopped and ate lunch with the Parkers. Andy and I have many memories of unicycling with Elijah. We trained with him for several unicycle tours Andy organized over the years. He was the photographer for our wedding. Less than a month after our wedding, we went to his wedding, celebrating his union with Jackie. Now they have five boys and homeschool them. It was enjoyable to catch up with them and glimpse their life.

Visiting with the Parkers

CRYSTAL LAKE, IOWA

Today is our 16th wedding anniversary.
At breakfast, I said to Andy, "We could go down to the dock and have a vow renewal." Andy jokingly replied, "A bowel removal?! Do you want to go first or second?"
I love how much Andy makes me laugh.

We spent two nights in rental cabins with our friends Sarah and her two boys, C and R, in Crystal Lake, Iowa. Our kids get along well, and it was refreshing to visit with Sarah, change the scenery, and play together. We've known each other for several years. I appreciate seeing how our children have grown and developed, and having the space and time to talk with Sarah about how we, as adults/parents/humans, have grown and evolved. Sarah makes an epic bubble mix that is still fun to play with, even with our oldest kids at age 9, and even Andy and I tried to catch a few bubbles. We shared the story with them about our time in Thailand: every night we had the option to watch a fire show on the beach from the bar next to our lodging, and those songs are stuck in our heads. I pulled up a few of them and played that music while we chased bubbles as the sun set. Sarah was even brave enough to play Charades! with us and the kids, which was enjoyable.

Andy on the dock looking out at
Crystal Lake

Our friend Sarah and our family

STILLWATER, MINNESOTA

September 8th
Today I completed the Square Lake Sprint Triathlon!

My friend Hannah joined as well, this being her first-ever race! It was fun to have a cheering team, with Andy, Matthew, and Hannah's family also cheering me on. The distance was a .5-mile swim, an 18.5-mile unicycle ride, and a 3.1-mile run. I was the first (and only) athlete to complete the race on a unicycle today. I contacted the organizer ahead of time to ensure it would be OK for me to ride one wheel.

I arrived wearing my winter jacket and neck warmer, knowing the water would be cold. I was surprised by how the cool water made it hard to swim fast, but I managed to swim the whole 0.5 miles without stopping. I rinsed off with warm water from insulated water bottles, then got into my unicycling gear. The unicycle ride felt a bit long since I was mostly solo, though I initially passed a few bicyclists on the hill. I ran at a good clip, averaging 12–14 miles per hour, and finished feeling strong, though my knees hurt during the run.

Throughout the training process, I learned that I enjoy a structured schedule to achieve a goal. I also learned that I enjoy lap swimming and found several pools and lakes around the metro to swim in. Next time, I would invest in a wetsuit to stay warmer during the swimming section.

Hannah and Irene with our finisher medals!

Starting the running portion

My awesome support person, Andy

NEW BRIGHTON, MINNESOTA

September 15th

I've been focusing on finding a new routine this week, now that my official training for that race has ended. I decided not to participate in the Twin Cities Marathon. My knees will be all the better for it, getting the time I need off from running and long-distance riding. I tried swimming yesterday at the Brooklyn Center community center pool and even used a float between my legs, since my knee was sore at first, even in the water. Swimming is a great cardio workout, and I plan to maintain it in the weeks ahead. I joined a 4-week yoga series with Tanya at the Devanadi Yoga Lake Harriet Spiritual Center.

I am reading, listening, and learning about Nonviolent Communication (NVC). I plan to host an online circle with my friend Inge from Punta La Barca Digital Nomad Hostel in Ecuador in a few weeks, where we will explore this topic further. Anyone can join; the idea is to create a space for people to connect around a topic, much like the feeling Inge and I (and others) had while sitting around the bonfire at Punta La Barca. Recently, I've been noticing my language around praise. Marshall Rosenberg, the creator of NVC, said it is a powerful tool for reconciliation and for learning to give thanks genuinely. At the end of one of Marshall's talks, a woman approached him and said, "You are brilliant." He said, "That's not helpful." He said that anyone willing to praise is just as willing to speak poorly; it is a judgment-based way of speaking. He asked the woman, "What exactly did I do that made you think I am brilliant?" She had to think for a moment, then said again, "This whole workshop is amazing!" Again, he said, "Thank you for telling me you think this workshop is amazing, but what exactly did I say that made you feel this way?" She looked through her notes and then pointed out a few sentences she had jotted down that resonated with her. Marshall said, "Now that is helpful, to know what it was that moved you." Later, he learned that she had an 18-year-old son she had never connected with, and left the workshop feeling she could learn to speak using NVC techniques so she could communicate with him.

Marshall speaks of expressing heartfelt gratitude by telling someone about something they did that enriched their life, made it more wonderful, how it made them feel, and what need it met. NVC is about speaking directly from the heart, focusing on needs, and avoiding praise as a way to coerce or make people dependent on others' opinions/views/judgments of them. I am amazed at how often I want to praise my daughter or others at unicycle practice in everyday life because I think it is helpful. It will take me a lot of practice to become better at using NVC.

Andy and Ani riding to the start of a parade to participate with the Twin Cities Unicycle Club. There were wild turkeys they went past to get to the lineup.

Andy and I after a body weight workout

September 20th

While playing UNO with Andy and Ani at Young Joni last Sunday, I had a sudden thought storm about how much I love playing this game with them. Quick flashes of memory passed through my mind—scenes from all the places we've played together. Most recently, at our favorite udon noodle bar in Fukuoka, Japan, where a picture Ani gave the owner now hangs framed on the wall.

I thought of Šibenik, Croatia, where Andy and Ani played UNO and invented a wild variation of the game: the winner got to decide something the other person had to agree to do. When Andy won, we went outside to explore the town on foot and somehow ended up playing hide-and-seek in a local cemetery. We accidentally scared two passersby when they stumbled upon Ani and me hiding among the tombstones.

I thought of the Mormon missionaries in Split, Croatia, whom we introduced to the game during a game night. There were so many rules by then that they sometimes thought we were making them up on the spot. And I remembered the Mexican restaurant in Hoi An, Vietnam, where the game went on for an absurdly long time.

I am always glad when I say "yes" to play. It's surprising how hard it can be to let go of the *should do* mentality and say "yes" to an invitation to play.

UNO playing inside
Young Joni

Family reflection photo outside Young Joni

September 23rd

We have one month and one week left in Minnesota before we start our slow travels again, kicking off in Italy. I'm scheduling things I want to do before we depart and organizing meetups with friends and family. We are also helping with house projects. Andy is helping Mike put some finishing trim up in the family room and basement, and I'm patching and painting a wall in the basement. My Dad will help me create a place to hang up unicycles and store them in an organized fashion downstairs.

Playing Corn Hole with Mike

We visited the AMC Mounds View Theater this past Saturday to see Inside Out 2, which we enjoyed. I was surprised to discover it is now a second-run movie theater, with tickets priced at only $5. It is still functional, but it looks so different from what I remember from childhood.

My mom, Ani, and I visited the Tao Organic Cafe and Herbery and saw Zip Zap Moya at the Children's Theater yesterday afternoon. They are a circus group from South Africa, and their skills were amazing. They also had one unicyclist in the show, which I cheered loudly for.

I haven't been taking as many photos lately; perhaps the change in weather and simply feeling more like we are living a regular life have led to a decline in my photo-taking. We have been eating well with many local organic veggies and fruits from our friends at Prairie Drifter Farm, Loon Organics, and Breezy Hill Orchard. I made a roasted cauliflower salad with red onions, lemon zest and juice, pistachios, and parsley, which we enjoyed so much that I made it again the same week. I also made my first batch of zucchini bread this week, and the zucchini harvest is still coming in.

Andy riding Trials at the U of MN

Irene, Kay, and Ani at the Children's Theater

September 30th

While snuggling with Ani before falling asleep last Friday night, Ani told me, "Today was like my dream come true." She was referring to the little black dog that stumbled upon Grandma Joan's home in the late morning. I saw it through the window and called to it. Then, I called for Ani. After speaking with the neighbors, Steve and Lorrie told us they found the dog in their garage and that it had a sibling that had already been caught and taken to the animal shelter. We offered to watch it until someone heard back from the animal shelter that they had time to intake the dog.

Lorrie saw how much Ani enjoyed caring for the dog, so she loaned us her cat carrier and even stopped by the town shelter to see if anyone was there. She gave the volunteer my number and asked her to call me when she was available to welcome the dog.

Ani with the dog outside of the animal shelter

Ani stayed with the dog, making it comfortable, and even doing some of her homeschooling math lessons nearby. We didn't need the cat carrier; by the time we received the phone call from the shelter, Ani was petting the dog and lifting it onto the makeshift dog bed she'd crafted from old bedding.

After dropping off the dog, tears fell, but slowly the day improved. Playing with milkweed seeds and taking things slow for a while afterwards helped lift her spirits. We also had delicious pizza from Jomas Hill Winery and ran into a few people we knew while sitting there, which was lovely.

We appreciated watching the stars out of the window before falling asleep, hearing the crickets, frogs, and Canadian Geese on the Lake.

The dog reunited with his sibling

October 7th

Instead of running the Twin Cities Marathon yesterday, I arranged for guests to join us for lunch and dinner. I love cooking for others, and sharing food is a way I show appreciation for fresh vegetables and the connections they foster. Even though I love this, there are stressful moments before guests arrive when it comes to getting the house in order and ensuring the food is prepared far enough in advance to make the final preparation and serving of the meal go smoothly.

Yesterday morning, I tried applying some of the skills I've been learning in Nonviolent Communication. When Andy and I spoke about something he wanted me to give my attention to, saying, "You should really be spending an hour on…." I responded, "Looking at my schedule for today, I can commit to spending 5–10 minutes on it before I go to bed tonight." I wanted him to review our finances and go through our health care re-enrollment forms, and I've been bothering him about it these past few days. He said he would look at the forms, and we agreed to try to finalize them by Monday. I spent 10 minutes last night, while Ani brushed her teeth, looking over the document Andy was working on. I have found it helpful to schedule time on my calendar or commit to small increments so the request feels doable rather than overwhelming. Ten minutes is easier than an hour. My mom wants to visit a museum and has been bringing it up with me often these past few weeks, so yesterday we got out our calendars and scheduled the museum visit for an upcoming afternoon.

Everyone helped in their own way to prepare the meals, and we enjoyed visiting with my Godparents for lunch and our neighbors for dinner. We learned about Turkish customs and are energized about our upcoming visit there this February.

Last weekend, we visited the RenFest for its final day. We brought Ani's friend, Elo, with us and walked around the fair. On the positive side, I enjoyed wearing fairy wings and eyeshadow and fitting right in. On the negative side, I was pretty stimulated throughout the visit, as I find it challenging for my brain to sort everything around me into categories. It was Oktoberfest weekend, so there were people dressed as Germans in cute outfits, people in black goth dresses, Renaissance outfits with men who looked like they were straight out of a Robin Hood story, and so much cleavage from women showing off their busts in corsets. It took me a few days to get rebalanced after the outing.

My shadow at the Ren Fest

Mike working in his garage workshop

October 13th

While walking through HarMar Mall, Ani spotted a brow-threading store. She asked me, "What's that?" I said it was for people who wanted to remove their eyebrow hairs using a threading technique. Ani said, "Why would you want to get your eyebrows removed?!?" I realized after she asked about the picture she was imagining, people walking around with no eyebrows, and started laughing out loud. I had to catch my breath, then explain to her that it was just for shaping them, since some people believe they are more beautiful that way. She smiled as well, realizing how bizarre beauty standards can be.

In my late teens, I went through my childhood crafts and told my mom that she could get rid of my embroidery floss and friendship bracelets. Over the years, I received one of the boxes and stored it at the farm until I found someone to give it to. This past week, we walked into the kitchen to find another box of embroidery floss, with "Irene's Embroidery Floss" painted in watercolor and outlined in my childhood handwriting. I realized the treasure awaiting us and called Ani to discover its contents together. Half of it was filled with bracelets I made as a child; some were completed, and some were half-finished. There were books teaching how to make embroidery bracelets, and floss waiting to be used. Ani has tried making one bracelet style this week and is interested in learning more. I thanked my mom for keeping it, even though I once told her to throw it out. It felt like a time capsule from my childhood had landed at the perfect time for my own daughter. What a gift.

We visited Hutchinson last week and saw several people from our past. I felt good about fostering those connections by spending time with them. Reflecting on our choice of lifestyle, I realize that experiencing life by traveling is rewarding when we have people to share our discoveries with.

I enjoyed listening to this podcast, THE GREATEST INSIGHTS INTO HORMONAL BALANCE AND WOMEN'S HEALTH, with Kate O'Donnell and Dr. Claudia Welch https://healwithkate.org/podcast

I have been cooking and baking. Here are some of the dishes I've made:
Cabbage wrapped bacon braised with root vegetables (beets, daikon, and regular radishes, carrots), and apples
Lulu's surprise cookies - cookies packed with nutrient-rich seeds, red lentils, and brown rice syrup
Gluten-free, sugar-free apple crisp for my mother-in-law
Butternut squash apple soup
Lentil Mushroom Quinoa Loaf (vegan meatloaf)
Thai curry coconut soup

Joan playing Bananagrams

Ani making a friendship bracelet

October 14th

Educational Philosophy / Homeschooling / Worldschooling

I have had the question several times over the past few weeks, "How is homeschooling going?" On the surface, it seems like an easy question to get to know you. Now I see it as asking "what is your educational philosophy and how do you define success for your child?" Whew. My short answer is, "We follow a math and reading curriculum every day throughout the year, sometimes missing days because of travel or other life commitments. We subscribe to Mark Rober's Build A Box and learn about engineering concepts. We listen to and read many books of varying subjects. We visit museums. We supplement our learning with our travels and the culture and surroundings where we stay. We use Duolingo to learn different languages and how to read music."

Issy from the StarkRavingDad Blog (https://www.starkravingdadblog.com/) asked us in his most recent email newsletter to define our definition of success for our child's education. Andy and I just spoke about this while eating breakfast together. For me, one definition of success is nurturing Ani's desire for natural learning. I have seen her spend hours working on a children's book, asking for help with spelling or using her portable device to look up words for proper spelling. She will often spend up to two hours on a single drawing. Recently, she created a birthday drawing for our neighbor Eser, who is from Turkey. For inspiration, we looked up the Nazar Boncuk, a blue-eyed amulet found around Turkey. It symbolizes the jealous and envious looks of others, which, according to popular belief, can cause various misfortunes to a person or their property. Turkish people believe this amulet protects its wearer from negative energies by absorbing them. Ani then drew the Nazar Bonuck onto an anime character's shirt, which she turned into a card.

I find it helpful to listen to podcasts by other parents who have their children out of school. Recently, I started listening to the Living Joyfully Podcast, and found this specific episode interesting about transitional ages and seasons:

https://livingjoyfully.ca/blog/2024/09/eu371-unschooling-stumbling-blocks-transitional-ages-and-seasons/
EU371: Unschooling Stumbling Blocks: Transitional Ages and Seasons

They talk about how at 9/10 years old, children become more aware of the world around them and want to retreat to a safe place. I have seen that with Ani. There have been major questions lately from her, often coming after reflection and rest, or bathing in a nice warm bath. She asked me, "What is the meaning of life?" and "Why is there war?"

On a practical level, in the State of Minnesota, there is also a requirement to have an annual standardized exam given by me or someone else. We have worked with a woman named Cindy who administers the Woodcock-Johnson test to Ani, which will tell me where she lands in grade level based on her responses. I am required to keep this record, and should Ani ever want to go to school, I would give her results to the school so they know where to place her. It also tells me which area Ani needs more help with and which area she is more advanced in. She will be taking her exam this afternoon. I am usually more nervous about it than Ani. I already have a good feeling about where she will land, but I will go through this to continue to follow the rules around home education in MN. I recently learned that our school district will also reimburse me for this fee, which is helpful.

Birthday card Ani made for our Turkish friend, Eser

163

October 19th

We have about two weeks left here in Minnesota. Every day counts; we are still trying to make space and time for family and downtime. This past week, we took Ani to visit the Minneapolis College of Art and Design to see their gallery and walk the halls a bit. It is on the list as a school Ani could attend for PSEO (Postsecondary Educational Options) when she is in 11th and 12th grade, and the state of MN would cover her tuition. We left as soon as Ani had seen enough, and we won't bring it up again, but we hope we planted a seed of an idea she may return to in the future.

Andy and I had a date night at the Moth Grand Slam Championship at the Fitzgerald Theater on Tuesday. I love attending the Moth performances. People tell stories that are from their own lives. I always leave having appreciated hearing about another person's life experience. Before the show started, I read the program, and one of the names listed felt familiar. I told Andy, "I think this is a cookbook author. I believe you gave me one of her cookbooks for Christmas when we were at the farm." Sure enough, Robin Asbell took the stage and started telling her life story about discovering how, as a teenager, being skinny made people notice her, then how anorexia made her body bloat and her mind turn to mush, then her research into whole foods and how what you eat affects your brain. She said she had written 11 cookbooks, and I knew I owned one. If you're interested in seeing them, you can visit: https://robinasbell.com/

I leave Moth Story Hour curious about the stories hidden in the strangers we pass every day. Someday, I hope to take the stage and share a story.

Thursday evening, Ani and I went to volunteer for Bare Bones, which is an annual Halloween outdoor puppet extravaganza, a community-created spectacle pageant of larger-than-life puppetry, drama, stilting, dance, fire, song, and music that honors the circle of life by celebrating its seasonal arc of death in the Fall. The puppets are being built inside the In the Heart of the Beast Theater in Minneapolis.

We walked through the door and were amazed to see all the puppets on the walls. After spending time with the people there, Ani and I were surprised by how friendly everyone was. They even made a beautiful dinner featuring whole foods, vegan, and vegetarian options, encouraging people to sit and share their meal. Ani and I helped one artist paper-mache pieces of grocery-bag paper onto a lily pad that will be held and used as a shadowbox during production. More info on the show can be found here: https://barebonespuppets.org/halloween-show/

Ani doing paper-mache

Visiting the MPLS College of Art
and Design

October 23rd

When Bob Walser invited me to the Bal du Nord, a French Folk dance he was organizing here in Minneapolis, a spark of gratitude for past connections lit inside me. Bob and Julie came to York Farm and were the square-dance callers for the Hoedown parties we held for several years in the fall, marking the transition from the busy harvest season in summer to the fall when one would traditionally put their hoe down. The last Hoedown was in 2014, when I was pregnant with Ani. I invited my childhood friend, Lindsay Holiday, to join me this week. We arrived, said hello to Bob and Julie, and started dancing. Random people took our hands, and after a pair dance, we joined a large circle and were led through a series of dances by Bob and other dance leaders.

When I tell people about our slow traveling lifestyle, I often get a response of them being excited and lit up about the possibility of travel. If that person has deep roots and a home, I think of the social connections they have worked toward and all they have in their present community. I sometimes find myself justifying our travel life and trying to help the person see what incredible bounty they have right here. I find it interesting how quickly humans discount the value of familiarity, routine, and the connections we share with those around us. I started reading Simple Abundance: A Daybook of Comfort and Joy by Sarah Ban Brethnach. She writes stories for every day of the year. On October 16th, the title is "Ceremonials for Common Days. ...We actually do most of our living among the common days, taking them for granted just the way we do the people we love. Yet myriad occasions during the course of each day cry out for consecration.

A liturgy of commonplace moments ripe for personal ritual might include sipping the first cup of coffee; putting on one's public face; eating at one's desk; window shopping; making a long-desired purchase; crossing the threshold at night; changing into comfortable clothes; hearing the sound of a loved one's homecoming footsteps; sitting down to a simple meal; being paid; traveling on business; sharing a laugh, or a confidence, or both; indulging in rainy day reveries; curling up to watch videos at home; sleeping late and having breakfast in bed; starting a good book; losing five pounds; having a good cry; and so to bed. There is no shortage of common day ceremonies to be enjoyed, only weary imaginations needing inspirational transfusions."

On Oct. 17th, she writes, "...But what if, as curators of our own contentment, we deliberately cultivated the habit of being: a heightened awareness of Real Life's abundance? The habit of being is a grateful appreciation for the good surrounding us, no matter what our circumstances might be today. What if you knew there was always going to be a simple pleasure to look forward to every few hours? What if you made sure there was? How do you think you'd greet the day?"

As we prepare to travel again, I find myself in a heightened state of awareness of the simple joys of everyday life here at my parents' home in New Brighton. I want to continue this practice wherever we are.

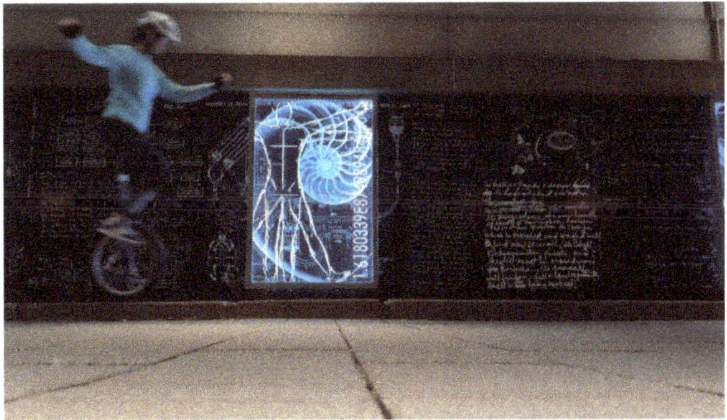

Irene unicycling at the U of MN during one of our regular Wednesday night meet ups

167

Ani getting a birthday waffle plate

Ani's Halloween costume

This year, instead of a party, we had a quiet day with friends and family, with downtime. We ate lunch at Chimborazo with one of Ani's friends.

I look forward to the years to come.

October 26th
Ani's 10th Birthday

I awoke yesterday to celebrate Ani's 10th birthday. My mother-in-law sent me a congratulatory text on my 10th year as a mother. When I think of it that way, it is worth celebrating. It has taken 10 years to start to get to know this person whom we welcomed into the world.

Marshall Rosenberg said, "If you want to know what my version of hell is, imagine that there is such a thing as being a perfect parent." I smiled when I heard this, because I have also learned there is no such thing as perfection. I am glad to have the opportunity to be Ani's mother, and embrace the learning journey along the way.

Trick or treating with Grandpa Mike answering the door

168

November 3rd

We watched the snow fall on Halloween. The wet, heavy flakes almost seemed to call me to watch them, to slow down and take in this season change. Ani stared out the window, then sat on a desk near it so we could do her homeschooling there, close to the falling snow. We completed Level D of RightStart Math by the window, after doing the lessons together most days this past year and a half.

While reading Simple Abundance: A Daybook of Comfort and Joy by Sarah Ban Brethnach, I found this passage from November 1st to be a good reminder of how the climate outside affects my well-being.

"There is a queen who is distraught each autumn as the year begins to ebb and falls into a deep melancholy. She calls upon her advisors to explain the cause of her baffling condition. After trying to speak with the court physician, the stargazer, the psychic, the alchemist, the herbalist, the philosopher, she finally finds comforting words when speaking to the gardener. He says, "Majesty, it is not your body or mind that is ailing. It is your soul that is in need of healing. While you are a mighty and powerful queen, you are not Divine. You are suffering from a human condition that affects us all. Earthly souls ebb and flow in sorrow and joy according to the seasons of emotion, just as the seasons of the natural world move through the cycle of life, death, and rebirth. These are the days to be grateful for the harvest of the heart, however humble it might be, and to prepare for the coming of the year's closure. Even now, the daylight season diminishes and the time of darkness increases. But the true Light is never extinguished in the natural world and is the same in your soul. Embrace the ebb, my beloved queen, and do not fear the darkness. For as night follows day, the Light will return, and you will know contended hours once again.""

Completing Level D in RightStart Math!

We saw Bare Bones' annual Halloween Extravaganza on Saturday night – an outdoor spectacle of giant puppets, fire, aerialists, and more. Ani and I saw the lily pad we helped papier-mache a few weeks ago when volunteering.

I am glad to be able to live our slow traveling lifestyle. One of the hardest parts for me is leaving a place we have stayed in for some time, because we leave the friends and family we have connected with behind. This transition feels especially tough, as we have been in Minnesota for four months, rekindled some great friendships, and made new connections. One morning this week, while eating oatmeal with my mom, I started crying, thinking about goodbyes. I am reminded of a saying around grief – that the feeling of sadness of losing someone is actually representative of the love that you felt with them. When viewed in this way, I feel so loved.

We are in transit to Italy and should arrive there on Nov. 4th. We have already cast our absentee ballots for the US presidential election. I am grateful for the right to vote, knowing that in some countries, residents lack it.

MILAN, ITALY

November 5th

Our first meal here was at Piz, a pizza restaurant recommended by our friend and wedding officiant, John Stone. It's right around the corner from our Airbnb. The staff there loved the music inside so much that they would break out and sing along. The decor was colorful, and the pizza had a delicious thin crust. If we were in the States, I would call this restaurant over-the-top with its decor and waiters, but here it felt like a perfect Italian experience.

Andy and Ani stayed awake through all the flights because sleeping on planes was too uncomfortable. I had some unsatisfactory sleep on our last flight from Dublin to Milan, the kind where you wake up every 5-10 minutes with a crooked neck. I purchased some breakfast oatmeal fixings at one of the local grocery stores, and even though I was carrying only a few items (no basket or cart), I had more than the average customer at checkout. It is common for Italians to go to the store daily to pick up one or two essentials.

We slept well, thanks to the Jet Lag.

We grabbed some sandwiches from a shop with fresh bread and fixings, then sat on the stone steps outside the shop for lunch. Some pigeons enjoyed the scraps and bits people gave them. I missed pigeons. We visited the Duomo di Milano, the Cathedral of Milan, today. We walked through the main building, admiring the gorgeous stained-glass windows depicting stories from the Bible. When I explained to Ani that in the past, not everyone could read, so they depicted the Bible's stories in the glass windows, Andy said, "There you go, just like graphic novels." We passed several saints whose mummified bodies are on display. We walked up the stairs to the top of the cathedral, Ani saying, "I love elevators," over and over. Andy said, "The good news is that if you die here, you can be put on display with the other saints." That was, of course, just for fun, and it made me smile.

I noticed how easy travel was on this trip; my anxiety about catching flights and the metro was very low. It helps that we have done this for so long and now know what to expect. Andy set up e-SIM cards on our phones at Dublin Airport while we waited for our flight to Milan, so that, upon touchdown, we could restart them and be connected right away. I enjoy people-watching here because the Italians are well-dressed when out and about. The last several months of Italian I have been studying on Duolingo have also helped me pick up on some words from conversations people have as we pass by.

Ani with pigeons!

Ani and Irene in front of the Duomo di Milano

November 7th

Yesterday, we visited Marco Vitale and Amedea Bruni at the Mad4One Unicycle Headquarters in Varese, Italy. Ani picked up her new 24" unicycle, our big birthday gift to her this year for turning 10. I got a carbon-fiber seat for our 20" urban unicycle.

Marco showed us a variety of unicycles for sale. I was able to test ride a few of them, even taking a lightweight carbon fiber wheel on a 36" for a 30-minute ride through town. They will typically make unicycles to order, choosing the proper parts to create the requested unicycle. While they do sell beginner unicycles, they focus on advanced models with lightweight components and high-quality materials that withstand heavy use.

Marco assembling my carbon-fiber seat

Irene trying out one of the many unicycles

I enjoyed learning more about Marco's past. Before starting Mad4One, he was big into sailing. He competed in sailing and worked at a company that crafted custom sails for boats. He also bred German Shepherd Dogs and worked in IT.

We went with Amedea and Marco to a famous pizza restaurant in Varese. The building's owner is also the president of the Italian Unicycle Federation. Some of the chefs at this pizza place have won awards for throwing pizza dough in the air. Marco said that some Italian unicyclists have also thrown pizza while riding their unicycles here.

We first met Marco and Amedea during the Mediterranean Unicycle Tour in 2007. They and several other Italian unicyclists met our group in Siena and organized a day at a local home, with a beautiful meal.

Group photo at our pizza dinner

November 10th

Friday morning, we left our Airbnb and walked to the metro, only to find the gates were closed. Andy led us across the street to the other side, where we could enter, but it was blocked off as well. We thought this stop might be undergoing maintenance, so we walked to the Duomo and found all the metro entrances blocked off as well. Then we realized we were experiencing a metro strike, something Andy had read about in the days prior, which was happening on Tuesday. We got in line for a taxi, which was quite long. I realized we would miss our train. Ani was anxious about missing our train, but once we reassured her that we could find another and that we weren't in a rush, she calmed down. How she feels is directly related to how well we handle the unexpected situation. We eventually got into a cab and had a pleasant, although slow, ride to the central train station, passing many people walking on the streets. Andy explained what a strike was to Ani. Traffic was higher than usual. We got another train ticket. The train company did not reimburse us for our first tickets. I believe our travel insurance will cover lost tickets due to strikes, but for 30 Euros, I'm not sure it is worth the hassle. We nearly missed getting off the train in time because the door we stood at to descend from was locked for some reason, so we hurried Ani through the train car to the next exit, and she hopped off just in time, with us following her.

Our friend Giuseppe welcomed us at the Torino (Turin) train station and brought us to his home. Barbara had cooked an excellent lunch for us, with lots of vegetables. When she asked if we preferred anything in particular, I asked for lots of veggies, since our diet lately has been heavy on pizza and focaccia. Giuseppe drove us in their RV to the RV park near Turin, and Barbara and Jacopo met us there to get us settled in for the night. This is our first time staying in a mobile RV as a family. It is a test run to see how we like it, as we will be traveling with 14 other families next fall for the Traveling Village 2 in campervans.

On Saturday, we met our friends in Turin at a pizzeria. We tried fried dough with tomatoes and greens and watched the chefs create pizzas and bake them in the wood-fired oven. We stopped into a cafe to admire the beautiful interior and have a warm beverage. We walked around Turin and found some geocaches together. We finished our visit with a hot chocolate, then headed home.

Our friend Giuseppe welcomed us at the Torino (Turin) train station and brought us to his home. Barbara had cooked an excellent lunch for us, with lots of vegetables. When she asked if we preferred anything in particular, I asked for lots of veggies, since our diet lately has been heavy on pizza and focaccia. Giuseppe drove us in their RV to the RV park near Turin, and Barbara and Jacopo met us there to get us settled in for the night. This is our first time staying in a mobile RV as a family. It is a test run to see how we like it, as we will be traveling with 14 other families next fall for the Traveling Village 2 in campervans.

On Saturday, we met our friends in Turin at a pizzeria. We tried fried dough with tomatoes and greens and watched the chefs create pizzas and bake them in the wood-fired oven. We stopped into a cafe to admire the beautiful interior and have a warm beverage. We walked around Turin and found some geocaches together. We finished our visit with a hot chocolate, then headed home.

Barbara, Giuseppe, Andy, Ani, and Irene about to eat a veggie heavy lunch

Meeting our friends!

November 12th

There is a YouTube Channel called Pasta Grannies
(https://www.youtube.com/user/pastagrannies) that has videos of
Italian grandmothers (and grandfathers) sharing how they make
pasta (and focaccia). Since I discovered it a few years ago, I
always thought it would be fun to meet a Pasta Granny. On
Sunday, I met Antonietta Santangelo, my adopted Pasta Granny
for the day. Our friend Giuseppe's mother, Antonietta, hosted
Giuppi, Barbara, Jacopo, Andy, Ani, me, and five other family
members at her home for a fresh-pasta class and a delicious
Italian lunch. Giuppi warned us about her personality and that her
life's goal is to feed people. She learned I was lactose intolerant, so
she found lactose-free mozzarella balls and parmesan, and the
tiramisu was even made with lactose-free mascarpone! She
served several courses with the help of Barbara and others,
bringing food to and from the kitchen. She made sure we were
eating, and when she saw what we liked, she would quickly and
expertly pop another piece onto our plate, almost without us
noticing. Then, when we did, we laughed and thanked her for the
food. We had antipasti, the traditional first course of a formal
Italian meal, to stimulate the appetite. The dishes included
mozzarella balls with cherry tomatoes and greens, sliced meats
sprinkled with olive oil and lemon juice, zucchini fritters, stuffed
roasted pepper slices with tuna and breadcrumbs, and another
meat tray. Then came the fresh pasta course with a slow-
simmered tomato sauce and parmesan. Then there was meat with
potatoes and mushrooms. Then she served fried eggplant with
melted mozzarella and tomatoes. Then they brought out the
tiramisù and apple-cinnamon galette. The whole meal lasted
several hours, with pauses in between courses. I asked once, using
Google Translate, if I could help clean up, and she quickly said,
"No!" and then enjoyed visiting with her family, leaving the piles of
dishes to be washed later.
I enjoyed watching the family interact and play together. Ani used
Google Translate to talk with a seven-year-old niece. They spent
time playing hide-and-seek in the garden with the older nephews.

At one point, Antonietta was on the couch by the fireplace with her youngest grandson, 11 months old, while swapping stories with Jacopo, 5 years old. She told him the story of Little Red Riding Hood, and Jacopo told her the story of Pinocchio.

Giuseppe warned us to leave before dinner; otherwise, she would start cooking again and insist we eat. She brought out fresh clementines later in the day, and the citrus felt good on the taste buds, balancing out the other food. We left with food packages, including the homemade pasta we made together and a jar of that special slow-simmered tomato sauce. Giuseppe said he knew his mother would love to host us and share a meal. I felt honored to be a guest in their home. What a gift to observe and receive hospitality of this level – the kind that gives meaning to life, to share good food with others.

Irene and Ani kneading pasta dough

Antonietta's hands shaping pasta

Tiramisu

November 14th

What I've learned from 5 days of campervan life:

*You use water efficiently for cooking. Having a sink to wash dishes outside the campervan is nice, even nicer when that water is hot, as it helps clean the dishes.
*Managing the water tanks (black, gray, and fresh) is interesting. When you know you will see the black water (toilet water) again when checking out of the campsite and dumping your tanks, you choose how often you use the campervan toilet and how often you walk to the toilet facility.
*You use water efficiently for showering if using the campsite facility. The two places we stayed required coins to operate the showers.
*When paying for electrical hookups, a space heater is a nice addition to the campervan, as you use less propane and it heats the small space quickly.
*You are very close to your family members. If one person wants to cook, the other person must be elsewhere. There is a lot of communication.
*Taking walks outside is a nice way to balance the closeness of the family inside.
*One person is outside the campervan helping the other back up when moving the van. If you can see the driver in the side mirrors, the driver can see you.
*Going slow while driving and looking for balconies, trees, and other low-hanging obstacles is worthwhile to prevent you from hitting them.
*Parking on a slope is OK for sleeping, but the doors for the cabinets then open and shut when you don't want them to!

Andy with the black water toilet disposal container, after emptying

Filling up the campervan

Dinner on the campervan stove

November 17th

My five-year-old Italian friend, Jacopo, reminded me to jump in
the leaves. Never pass up a ledge that is easy to balance on. Take
off your shoes whenever you can. Savor good, hot pasta and pizza.
Offer puppet shows frequently to whoever will accept your gift of
showmanship.

Barbara and Giuseppe brought us to the Italian coast and shared
their home in Cenesi. On Friday, we stopped at a rocky beach with
focaccia for lunch. Upon walking onto this beach, the sound of the
waves made me feel as if I were entering a relaxation soundtrack.
The sun warmed up our bodies enough for the kids to enter the
water and swim. Rock cairns were made. Jacopo asked for a story,
and I enjoyed listening to Barbara and Giuppi take turns, each
entering their imagination to create one for him as they lay on the
beach, cuddling. I didn't understand the Italian words, but hearing
them was comforting.

We enjoyed sharing pasta for dinner most evenings with our
friends. Last night, we tried to make wood-fired pizzas with
moderate success. The first time in a new place and with a new
oven made it hard to make the best pizza in the world, but as
Giuppi reminded me, it was an enjoyable process, and it was
made by hand by us! Here in Italy, they use special pizza flour and
pizza yeast.

Playing at the beach

Jacopo giving us a
puppet show

Giuppi with one of our
wood fired pizzas

November 18th

I automatically said, "Wow, that is beautiful," as Alberto, my free walking tour guide to Florence, brought our group to the Cathedral of Santa Maria del Fiore. The facade of this church is made from three different colors of marble, the most prized being white, which famous sculptors used to carve works such as Michelangelo's David.

The Ponte Vecchio has houses lining it, now filled with jewelry shops. During the Black Death in 1347–1348, people realized that rats carried the disease, so they had all the butchers live in the houses on the bridge. They could dump their offcuts and waste directly into the river to reduce rodents.

The Strozzi Palace displays two installations. The first, called Drift, explores the movements of the natural phenomenon known as nyctinasty, in which certain species of flowers and plants close at night and reopen at dawn to defend themselves and preserve their seeds. Watching the flower–like structures rise and fall to the music is beautiful. The second installation is by American painter Helen Frankenthaler, called Painting Without Rules. She created large paintings that were purposefully left abstract, as they could mean different things to each viewer. I enjoyed reading the program and learning about her life, her residences, her friends, and how she continued to paint wherever she lived. She was known for saying, "There are no rules" regarding art.

The Ponte Vecchio

November 23rd

I aimed to soak in as much art as possible while in Florence. I went to a museum every day, except the day we had three separate calls with families from around the world who were in the process of joining Traveling Village 2.

In museums, I would take pictures of art that I found stunning, or of specific details I wanted to remember or to show Ani. We did go to the Galleria dell'Accademia di Firenze together as a family and admired Michelangelo's famous statue of David. It was a small museum, so we walked quickly through it, seeing all the religious paintings and plaster casts used to create larger marble statues. Outside the Uffizi Gallery stands a replica of David, beside a statue of Hercules and Cacus, sculpted by Baccio Bandinelli. My tour guide pointed out that Michelangelo had studied anatomy because the body of David is more anatomically correct than that of Hercules. Hercules has extra muscles on his body that don't exist in Humans: too many abs and extra muscles in his legs around his knees.

Andy and Ani in Florence

Artwork by Ani

I wanted to bring Ani to the Uffizi, a well-known museum with free entry for students, and many Italians come to Florence to see it. But I knew her attention span wouldn't last very long, and she wasn't interested, so I went alone and took pictures of special pieces to share with her. My attention span lasted only through the top floor, with so much art in the museum. On the way to the exit, I had to walk past the Caravaggio gallery and was surprised at some of the graphic and provocative pieces that Caravaggio painted. A man with snakes for hair, and another of someone cutting a man's head off with lots of blood. This was when I realized I had made the right decision to go alone to the Uffizi, as this kind of art would make a big impression on Ani and may cause nightmares. I learned from a past experience bringing young Ani to an art museum: ask the staff before entering whether there are any pieces not suitable for young eyes.

We rented an apartment with excellent reviews and a cozy feel. I asked our host in advance to remove any air fresheners, and she did. It was comforting to have a consistent place for five nights with a good kitchen to cook in. After two days of mediocre dining out, we cooked all our meals in the kitchen on our last day.

Looking up at the tower on the main square in Siena

Irene putting Ani's uni together after arriving in Siena

November 24th

Our Airbnb host met us and welcomed us into her well-lit apartment on the top floor, four flights of stairs from ground level. Like the other hosts we've met here in Italy, she was well dressed, wore makeup, and had her hair styled. She was very outgoing and friendly, even stocking the fridge and pantry with the basics for breakfast and a few pasta meals.

On our first day here, I was tired. Transitions from city to city, even if only 1.5 hours by train, take a lot of energy from me. I awoke early for a call with a New Zealand family planning to go on TV2. Yesterday I decided to listen to a yoga nidra meditation and take a short nap, despite the beautiful sunshine coming into the apartment. I awoke feeling more alive, and I went out to explore the streets of Siena before sundown. In a good portion of the city, traffic is limited, making exploring on foot pleasant. I searched for two geocaches without any luck. I stopped into several stores, looking at the contents inside. In three different stores, at three different times, friends of the workers stopped in to say hello and chat while they were behind the till. It makes me believe this city is alive, with locals among all the shops and restaurants.

We first visited Siena in 2007 for the Mediterranean Unicycle Tour. We met up with a group of Italian unicyclists and had a rest day here, staying for two nights. It is nice to be back in this city and to be able to stay for 12 days, enjoying the slower pace.

The front of the Siena cathedral

November 27th

We have been exploring something new daily in the walled city of Siena. I have been cooking most of our meals at home. We homeschool, take phone calls, and plan for the upcoming Traveling Villages. I am trying to commit to doing some art with Ani every day. We listen to audiobooks together, and I always feel better after I take this time, though it can be hard to start.

We explored Siena Cathedral, an ornate building whose contrasting marble colors make you think of optical-illusion illustrations. There are many sculptures both inside and outside. In front is a she-wolf, which is a symbol of Siena. The legend is that Siena was established by Senius, son of Remus and nephew of Romulus. Therefore, Siena's symbol is a she-wolf nursing Romulus and Remus. The symbol has been repeated in different parts of town and art pieces.

We learned about the Palio, a horse race typically held twice a year in the big central square. There are photos from the race, horse heads, and horse paintings around the town. At night, Ani likes to grab an evening snack outside our apartment, and we usually head to the large square. Sometimes we play tag. Last night, we completed our first Adventure Lab Geocache by visiting different parts of the square and answering questions in the app. I have been searching for geocaches as well, which has taught me a lot about the city, as cache owners often include historical information in their descriptions.

The main square that holds the Palio

Ani and Andy in our apartment

December 1st – Julio Le Parc at Palazzo Delle Papesse di Siena –

Julio Le Parc is an Argentine-born artist who focuses on modern art and kinetic art. Le Parc attended the School of Fine Arts in Argentina. A founding member of Groupe de Recherche d'Art Visuel and an award-winning artist, he is a significant figure in Argentine modern art.

We visited his exhibit at the Palazzo Delle Papesse in Siena, Italy, yesterday. It was one of my favorite experiences at a modern art gallery. He had a variety of artworks that delighted the senses. One room had so many small dots that it made you appreciate the sheer amount of time it would take to patiently dot each one on the canvas, and then you saw how they blended in color to create a big, beautiful piece. In another room you walked into, a docent suggested you use your phone, as you could see the piece differently through its lens. Indeed, the illusion became apparent when looking through the phone's photo viewfinder. She said you could also experience it if you looked at the piece for a minute. A virtual reality headset featured a virtual gallery of art that you could "walk" through. He had dark rooms with lights and different art pieces hooked up to machines, moving metal pieces around in front of the artwork to create a visual feast for the eyes. As you walked past a piece of art with metal in front of it, you saw how the colors bounced off the metal and created reflections. This was one exhibit that I felt you really couldn't replicate using video or photos. It required your presence to experience it fully. You can search for Julio Le Parc and see many of his art pieces on Google Images. Have you ever experienced an art exhibit like this? One you can't quite put into words, or that needed you to be present to experience it?

December 2nd

My free walking tour guide explained the rich history of the Palio Horse Race in Siena. There are 17 contrade (city wards) in Siena, each represented by an animal or a natural symbol. There are 17 fountains, one for each contrada. If you have a child that you want baptised, you would do so using the water from this fountain. There are small balls that children play with called barberi, each painted in a different pattern to represent a different contrada. Some believe the games they play with them may predict the winner of the next Palio race. Before the race starts, the horses walk into the church of their contrada for a blessing. The jockeys ride the horses bareback, and it is common for a few jockeys to fall off during the race around the town square. Having the jockey on the horse isn't required for your horse to win the race. The winner receives an honor and a hand-painted silk banner or palio, designed by artists from around the world. The winning district has its flag displayed throughout town until the next race.

We have befriended pizzeria owners Paolo and Antonella, who are down the street from our apartment. Usually, Ani and Andy stop by in the evening on their way out to explore before bed and grab a small snack. Last Thursday, we decided to go to a different restaurant, since it was Thanksgiving in the US and we wanted to celebrate with an evening family meal. We went to the local pizzeria on Friday evening, and Paolo said, "I'm sorry, did you see the note?" Then he showed us a hand-printed note. He forgot to tell Andy and Ani on Wednesday that he would be closed on Thursday, so he left a note for them in their shop window. Ani has been gifting him artwork, and he has gifted her chocolate and a magnet with Siena printed on it and Barberi balls of the 17 different contrada below it. It is sweet to develop this friendship in our local neighborhood.

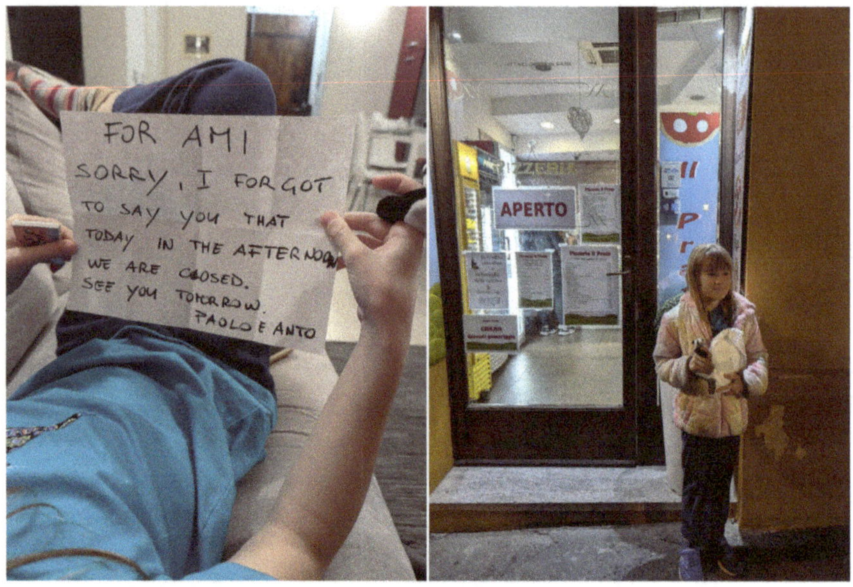

The note that Paolo and Anto left for Ani

Ani outside the Pizzeria with her evening snack

Ani unicycling in "The Turtle," a covered space for a farmer market

Irene's shadow

I visited the municipal swimming pool on Sunday morning to try lap swimming. I rode my unicycle there (about 5km) and then swam for 30 minutes. I am trying to heal a few overuse injuries in my knees and arm, and I wanted to see how swimming felt. I was a bit nervous, given the language barrier and the fact that I had never been to this pool before. In Italy, they require swimming caps, and I got a card that activated the shower and hair dryer, which I paid for separately at 0.20 euros each.

Admission was only 6 euros. I ended up chatting with a few other swimmers when I asked if I could share lanes with them, and it was interesting to talk. One was an athlete from Greece who had lived in Italy for 10 years. He said that in Greece, people have to learn to speak English, and he said that more and more Italians are learning to speak it. Another was an older Italian woman. I told her that in the States, they don't require swim caps, and she said, "There, they must be so modern with a better water filtration system." I don't know if that is the reason, but I found the perspective of someone from Italy, rich in history and older buildings, putting American modernity in the spotlight interesting. How one sees the world truly reflects what they have around them. This is another reason I enjoy traveling. I always evaluate how cultures function and what I view as beneficial or beautiful. The swimwear here is different for men as well. Every man was sporting a Speedo, no matter their shape or age.

One of Ani's art pieces created in Siena

December 6th

Delights:
*It is easy to buy organic produce and source healthy foods and treats
*Romeow Vegan Cat Bistro, with haute vegan cuisine and seven house cats that you can interact with
*Free Walking Tours. Mine was about the artist Caravaggio. Did you know that he didn't have a lot of money, so he would often use prostitutes and friends as models? He also cut a hole in the ceiling of his rental apartment to let in good-quality light for painting. He got in trouble with the landlord and never paid to fix it. He became well known through his connections with a prominent figure in Rome, showing that even in ancient times, networking and friendships mattered. He brought biblical stories to life and dressed his characters in contemporary clothing, which appealed to his present-day audience.
*Eating lunch on the apartment balcony at lunchtime and listening to pleasant street music being played.
Not so delightful:
*101 steps to reach our fifth-floor walk-up apartment (I will say the steps are marble and in good shape, so at least the walk is beautiful for the eyes)
*Noisy streets outside our apartment, which interrupt our sleep
*It took 24 hours to figure out how to get the apartment heated up properly.

     At Romeow Cat Bistro

Enjoying a meal on our balcony

At Romeow Cat Bistro

December 10th

My friend Tom Blackwood wrote to me suggesting I visit the Ponte
Sant'Angelo and the Castel Sant'Angelo. He also shared a TED Talk
by an acquaintance that explores the architectural wonder of the
Ponte Sant'Angelo and its angel sculptures. On Sunday afternoon, I
walked to see these sites. I left after a big rain shower passed
through the area, admired the Ponte Sant'Angelo, and arrived at
the ticket office for the Castle 5 minutes before a tour was
planned to leave, so I said, "Yes, I'd like to join." An enthusiastic
archaeologist tour guide took me and four others on an hour tour
of the Castle, explaining its many uses over the years. Initially, it
was built as Hadrian's tomb, with yellow marble lining the walls and
fine mosaic inlays on the floor (only brought to life through
storytelling, as most of the marble has been pillaged over the
years). It has served as a prison and, most recently, a safe place
for the Pope to escape in times of war and crisis. Our guide
pointed out the narrow pathway that leads from Vatican City to
this Castle. At the end of the tour, she left us outside a hall that
was just about to start a swing concert. I walked inside and
marveled at the beauty of the walls, the upbeat music, and my
luck in timing the afternoon so well, with the clear weather, a good
tour guide, and a fun concert. Also, having a friend like Tom, who
suggested this excursion. I wonder – am I ever alone in a big city
when I can stay connected to friends and family online?
We venture out once or twice a day to savor delicious Italian food,
visit Christmas Markets, and take in the sights. I am grateful we
can be here for 12 days to slow down the process of trying to see
many things. Sometimes I am glad to eat out, and other times I am
so happy for our kitchen and the ability to eat healthy veggies that
are often lacking in restaurant food.
It is human nature to feel homesick when traveling. I am learning to
coexist with this feeling, knowing it is there. I can reach out to
family and friends with the fast, high-speed internet and video
chats. I am learning to focus on things other than missing out or
the guilt of not being somewhere else.

The weather has been rainy these past few days. On the plus side, the loud seagulls that sound like fighting cats during the night outside our bedroom window haven't been making much noise in the rain. There can be some beautiful stormy skies and light when the rain passes. I also feel OK spending more time inside when it rains, which helps me tamp down on the feeling of missing out on all of the possible Roman ruins I could see.

The Ponte Sant'Angelo and the Castle Sant'Angelo

December 12th

Ani and I went to an exhibit titled The Art of Play, where there were movie screens showing animations, larger-than-life teddy bears to cuddle, a Barbie-sized dollhouse with a ball pit, and more plastic things meant to spark joy. I felt silly being there. Ani and I talked about what play looks like to us. Why do people pay money to be surrounded by these play-type things? It felt like an experience that helped me close the chapter of going to these types of exhibits. While walking to the bus stop, we passed a hair salon with a cute dog in the window, which Ani interacted with through the glass. I used Google Translate to ask the woman working there if she would have a few minutes to give Ani a bang trim, and she said she did. So, we went inside and petted the dog named Nini, and Ani got a bang trim. When I took out my wallet to pay her, she said, "NO! Sono stati solo pochi minuti." (No, it was only a few minutes!) I said, "Grazie mille," and we left.

On Wednesday, we visited the Colosseum. This was the main reason we came to Rome, as Ani said she would like to see it someday. It is massive. It has a somber feeling when you realize all of the lives lost there (both human and animal) in the gladiator battles in years past. Walking up the stairs required you to lift your feet slightly higher than usual, as the stairs were also taller than your average step. It started to rain. Men selling ponchos and umbrellas flocked to the tourists standing outside the entrance. I saw two men hop off the metro and run to the tourists, not wanting to lose those perfect moments just after the rain started, when they could help people stay dry and buy their goods. I purchased an umbrella, bargaining it down before handing over Euro coins. Thanking the man and feeling grateful to stay dry on my walk home.

I have seen several times the carabinieri, a branch of the Italian police, closing off streets for official-looking black cars with tinted windows to drive past on their way from one location to the next. There are loud warning bells, flashing lights, and a swift, serious feeling that comes when these cars drive past. I wonder who is inside. What would it be like to live a life where you need a secret service to escort you?

The Colosseum

Today we visited Vatican City. We arrived at 1:40 pm to find a sign outside St. Peter's Basilica stating that the last entrance of the day was at 1:30 pm. So, we took a photo, and Andy and Ani went back. I decided to see the Sistine Chapel. I hadn't done much research on it, but figured I could quickly walk there, visit the chapel, then return home so Andy could get outside while there was still sunlight, as today is one of the few dry, sunny days this week. Boy, was I mistaken about the 'quickly walk there' part.

There was no line for museum tickets, which I appreciated, but I started walking and couldn't find it easily, so I had to ask a couple of guards for directions. Then I realized I had to walk through several museums to the Sistine Chapel. There were so many beautiful pieces of art. I took pictures of a few that I found amusing. In one area, there were detailed marble statues or busts every two feet. There was a hall of maps—a hall of intricately woven rugs. Then, finally, I arrived at the Sistine Chapel. I sat for a while looking at the ceiling. The conversations around me were amusing to listen to.

A young couple speaking to each other, in that phase of the relationship where they were getting to know each other and feeling awkward. I learned she loves it when boys touch her hair. She tried to explain the Sistine Chapel ceiling to him. He said he wrote about the very thing she described in his report on the paintings. It made me appreciate the stage of my relationship I'm in now, the knowledge I have of Andy's likes and dislikes, and how he knows mine. I finally exited the Vatican Museum and walked home, too late for Andy to get outside in the sunshine. I lay down and took a quick power nap, letting all the images and beautiful things my eyes took in settle in my body and mind.

Outside the Vatican

December 14th

On Friday, Andy and I explored St. Peter's Basilica. You can walk all the way to the top of the dome to look out over the city. There are over 500 stairs to the top. Andy went first, then came back, and later that afternoon, I went out, walking through rain showers to visit the Basilica. The walk up to the top features some very narrow passages, and toward the very top, the dome structure forces you to lean far to the right to continue upward. Being at the top made me think about how small we humans are, and how large Rome is. I walked down into the basilica and was blown away by the opulence and artwork. I admired the large artworks at first, thinking they must be paintings, but then realized they were all large, ornate mosaics. There were pieces of marble that looked like cloth. In the center of the building is a large, Baroque-sculpted bronze canopy that, at first glance, resembles a dark Brazilian Cherry Wood sculpture. It was overwhelming to imagine how much effort and cost went into creating this vast space.

Taken while walking around Rome

December 15th

I found Giulia at BLocal Travel (https://www.blocal-travel.com/) and arranged a private tour with her to explore Rome's street art. Seeing Street Art the day after visiting St. Peter's Basilica was an interesting contrast regarding how long a piece of art lasts. She has a wealth of knowledge about Street Art in Rome and across the world. She lived in Amsterdam for four years, helping to open the STRAAT Street Art Museum. She and her partner organize trips that take interested people to different European cities to view street art together. I encourage you to visit some of the websites below for examples of these artists' work.

Artists:

Vhils – Alexandre Farto – (https://vhils.com/en/about)
His work really surprised me in the way he removes existing materials (walls, rocks, poster boards) to create an image. Check out this video https://tinyurl.com/5n98jfbr for his tribute to the Portuguese Author José Saramago. His approach to art still moves me, and I look forward to learning more about him and his work.

Sten Lex – https://stenlex.com/
This artist has changed their style over the years. Giulia said they had a big mural of a famous football player on one building in Rome. It was beloved by many because they loved that football player. Over time, it needed to be redone, so the neighborhood launched a crowdfunding campaign to bring them back and paint another mural. They created an artwork on the building that, when first completed, was all black. Over time, as wind, rain, and the elements struck the wall, pieces of it fell off, revealing a new geometric/abstract design. Some people may have been disappointed, expecting a football player. Others may have seen it as an interesting way to use the elements, paired with street art, to bring a new art form into the world. This also showed the Roman government that Street Art was valued and helped open minds to future large-scale projects.

C 215 – Christian Guémy – http://www.c215.fr/en/c215-5/
C 215 went through a divorce and was missing his daughter. He made a stencil portrait of his young daughter (she looks to be around 8 years old), and to let her know he was thinking of her, he put up this street art stencil around her school and the area she frequents. This portrait has become well-known around the world.

Alice Pasquini – https://www.alicepasquini.com/
She signs her work with her real name, Alice, hoping to encourage other women to create Street Art as well. She portrays women not as sexy bodies.

Invader – https://www.space-invaders.com/home/
He places tiled frescoes around cities worldwide. He calls himself a street artist, graffiti artist, and game maker. You can download an app and try to find his art pieces worldwide. My guide, Giulia, helped him touch up some of his tiled work. She and a small team went out at night, with Invader's permission, to fix his work. She said she spoke to Invader's wife to get the kind of tile he used for the specific art piece, since they keep records of what was used and where the frescoes were placed.

Guido Van Helten – https://guidovanhelten.com/
He has some fantastic work on large silos as well, which you can see on his website.

Alex Senna – https://www.alexsenna.com.br/
He is colorblind, so he only paints in black and white. I love the way he incorporates shadow and fantastical birds into his work.

I took many pictures of these artists' work. Through the process of creating this book, I learned about copyright and how frequently street artists have their work reprinted without permission. In lieu of sharing their photos here, I encourage you to check out their websites.

LUXOR, EGYPT

December 19th

We arrived in Luxor, Egypt, on Tuesday. Our flight had several delays, but we finally arrived at the airport at 1 am, and Sayed welcomed us and drove us to our apartment for the next two months. On the first day, my body was tired and my mind muddled. I know it is just travel. I heard many unfamiliar noises around me, but we started to feel more comfortable in our surroundings as we walked into town to find a restaurant for lunch and groceries. People here will say, "Welcome. You are welcome here," as we pass. Most people are very friendly. Some will hassle you for a taxi or some money for food, but with a polite, "la shukran" (no), they leave you alone. We discovered a delicious vegetarian art café with its own resident cat, Rosy. I stopped at a spice shop to get supplies for the kitchen, and found so many things in the one small shop.

The owner is named Osman. I went to pay him and realized I didn't have enough cash, so he told me, "Don't worry, we are neighbors, come back later." Then handed me all of the groceries and sent me on my way. I came home to show Andy the bounty of pantry staples that I had amassed, and then I got some more cash at the ATM. I returned to pay Osman and continued searching for groceries.

Yesterday, Ani and I visited the Egyptian Adventures Worldschooling Hub. We spent the day there. We met Liana in person for the first time, along with all the coaches who help run the program. They were kind enough to feed us all breakfast and lunch. We went to a shop to buy galabeyas, traditional loose-fitting ankle-length robes with long sleeves and pockets. Then we visited a shop that makes scarves and watched the weaving unfold. We all left with scarves draped over our comfortable galabeyas.

Today at the hub, Ani and the children helped make bricks for the wood oven they want to create and install for New Year's. The mud was prepared yesterday and needed time to rest before it could be shaped into bricks.

I crossed the Nile to the East Bank to visit the supermarket and pick up a few specialty items I couldn't source locally.

I was asked a lot if I needed a ride or a taxi. One child even asked me for money for food, and I politely declined. I felt very sad about this, but I didn't want to support her asking random strangers this way. When I got to the other side of the Nile, it was common for Egyptian men to approach foreigners and say, "I work in your hotel! Remember me? I make the bread!" to try to build a connection and earn that person's trust. I politely declined, finally saying to one man, "I'm not living in a hotel." He said, "Oh, sorry." Then I kept walking. While there is some harassment, I feel safe here. The majority of people feel welcoming. I found an unscented plug-in for mosquitoes, and last night I slept soundly. I am a former organic farmer, so the idea of using pest spray isn't appealing to me, but it did help keep a few mosquitoes out of my room, for which I am grateful.

Ani and Irene in their galabeyas and scarves

Ani and Rosy cat

December 21st

https://grateful.org/

This website features a video I try to watch every morning as part of my morning routine. It helps me remember all the things I have around me to be grateful for.

I am learning that it takes constant practice to look for what is going well, because my natural tendency is to focus on the bad. It is much easier to complain and wish things were different than they are.

Brother David Steindal Rast, the creator of this website, uses the phrase "Stop. Look. Go" to remember to stop at any moment of the day, look for something in front of you to be grateful for, and continue on. He says you don't have to be grateful for hardships or sickness, but even in these trying times, if you look, you will find something to cherish.

For me, in our first week here in Egypt, our water supply from the Nile stopped working the other day. I wanted to try making some nut butter balls, which are sticky and would leave a mess on the kitchen counter. I worried about the ants that frequent the kitchen and if I could clean up the mess before going to sleep. I decided to be grateful that I had sourced all the ingredients and went for it. Thankfully, not much later, the water started working again, and I could clean things up. Our water isn't drinkable from the tap (my foreign microbiome isn't used to it yet), but it runs and gets hot.

Ani helping with the mud brick for the fire ring

Exploring the East Bank for the large grocery store

December 23rd

I made sweet potato brownies using Egyptian dates, which I hydrated and turned into a paste with my newly purchased immersion blender. Midway through the process, the power went out, so I considered pivoting and not incorporating the sweet potatoes because I couldn't blend them into the batter. They were cooked in small cubes. I continued with the other ingredients (including tahini for the nut butter, since it is common here), and by the time I gathered everything into the bowl, the power had come back on. I could blend them into a paste and add them to the dough. The oven is propane-powered and has two markings: low and high. I set the oven to medium and checked the brownies every 10 minutes. I started smelling something burning, but inserting a knife into the center of them proved to me they weren't cooked through. Then I realized the bottoms were burning. So I let them cool, then cut off the burnt bits on the bottom and sides, and they tasted good.

Today I tried to find a hair dryer, as I dislike going to bed with wet hair when nighttime temperatures are 40°F (around 5°C). I walked into a sports shop to find a baseball cap for Andy as a Christmas gift. The single hat they had wasn't what I was looking for, but I decided to ask the man for help finding a hair dryer. He thought for a minute, asked me where I was staying, and when I told him near the new bus station, he said, "Go to the bicycle shop, and go to the second floor and ask for a hair dryer." He spelled the name in English, "Gyoker," then in Arabic on paper and sent me on my way. I walked to the bicycle shop, saw the man who was always asking me to rent a bicycle as I passed by, and showed him the slip of paper. He welcomed me upstairs, as it was also his "Joker " shop. I carefully walked up the stairs, paying close attention to each step, as some were loose with several layers of cut-up carpet pieces arranged on top of them, and arrived on the second floor, where he sells household goods and cell phone items. He had his employee fetch me two hair dryers, and we set a price for the one I liked best. I negotiated down a little bit, and he accepted right away. This is a sign I should have negotiated a lower starting price.

His nickname is Hero, and he said, "I see you walking by and hustle you to rent a bicycle." I said, "Yes! We will rent a bicycle someday soon. But you should have said, 'want to buy a hair dryer?'" Then he offered to help me if I needed anything and tried to sell me a hot-air balloon ride. They wiped the box clean of the desert dust and put it into a shopping bag for me to take home.

We had a picnic in our front garden last Saturday afternoon with another family attending the Hub. This family has a single mom and six kids. She has been here since September and has many connections with the locals. She called an " Africa " restaurant and arranged for the owner to deliver food to us in the garden. It was nice to be together, eating outside, to have a chance to get to know her and her kids better. It was also lovely to be so close to home so that the kids could go back to their apartments when they needed to rest or use the washroom.

Liana also invited us to a rooftop sunset dinner on Saturday. We went up and enjoyed the setting sun while chatting with several other people.

When I smell the air outside, it often smells of smoke from burning things (trash? Green waste?), sweet-smelling shisha smoke from the men smoking the hookahs, and dust from the desert. Walking through our flower garden, I smell the scent of roses. Every day, I try to stop and smell at least one. In the morning, I hear birds chirping as they flitter about in the trees in our garden. Today, I saw birds flying in the air that looked like swallows.

Sign for the worldschool hub

Chocolate and plain sweet potato brownies

December 25th

Christmas isn't celebrated in Egypt. The big holiday is Ramadan, which falls in March this year. It made me feel a little discombobulated, unsure how to act around this traditionally big family day. I found myself walking the streets last night, looking for last-minute Christmas gifts for Andy and Ani. I walked about a mile, weaving in and out of traffic, to find a store that sold a hat for Andy, as he had forgotten his and wanted one. I found a knock-off Nike cap for $4. I purchased a few snack bags of chips and savory items blessed with the Egyptian desert dust from a small convenience store for Ani. I wrapped them in the plastic bags they use to wrap items (I'm always a few seconds too late pulling out my reusable shopping bags in these stores). I prepared for Ani an audio recording of her birth story, as she frequently asks me to tell it to her before bed.

This morning, I awoke at 4:45 am to join another family from our apartment building for a hot-air balloon ride. I have wanted to do this since 2010, when we visited New Zealand for UNICON (Unicycling Internationals). 22 companies run hot-air balloon rides here, and the streets were lined with white buses to collect passengers. The buses must enter the launch area simultaneously. There were 50 balloons launched this morning. I smiled the entire ride. It was so peaceful and smooth in the basket. There were moments of fear, mainly before takeoff, when everyone seemed to be yelling at each other to get the balloon oriented just right and to attach all the straps and pulleys to the basket. I reassured myself that everything would be fine, and it was. It helped me to know that Andy was with Ani, so if I died, my life insurance policy would kick in, and they would be fine. The landing was probably the scariest part. We crouched, holding the basket ropes, and then the ground crew met us to steady us as the balloon deflated. The pilot can't steer, only make the balloon go up and down, and the van drivers watch them from the ground, driving toward them to be able to collect the balloon and passengers as soon as they land. The hardest part was saying no to the children, who then flocked to the landing site, begging the passengers for money or trying to sell them items. The tour operators asked us not to engage with them.

We opened our presents around the makeshift Christmas tree Ani crafted with pillows, chairs, a sheet, homemade decorations, and a red Egyptian scarf. We went for lunch to Memnon Restaurant, eating across from the Colossi of Memnon. In ancient times, the statues became famous for their "singing" sounds. These sounds are said to have happened at dawn when the wind passed through the statue's mouth. They were damaged in earthquakes between 14 and 16 AD, which stopped the singing. We played cards, ate tagines, and tried Om Ali, a famous Egyptian dessert made with cream and puff pastry (I thank the lactose tabs from Italy for allowing me to try some).

I decided to ride my unicycle on the street today for the first time since arriving in Egypt. People were very positive, offering me many kind remarks. "Good driver" was often said, and I waved at the children, women, and men intrigued by me. On my way back from the restaurant, a tuk-tuk driver asked my permission to take a video of me riding. I said, "Sure. Thank you for asking." I think this is the first time anyone has ever asked before starting to film or snap a photo of me unicycling on public streets. He followed me for almost a mile, then, when I stopped to get off the main road, he asked if I wanted the video. We exchanged numbers, and he sent them to me. I have an offer for tea and sincere messages from him on my phone.

Liana arranged for us to visit with her artist friend Hamed at his home. We met Liana and Adel and drove to Hamed's humble home. He doesn't have a kitchen; instead, he eats at restaurants or has friends bring him food to share. He works in clay and stone. The clay comes from his home village. He sketches his ideas first, then crafts them into beautiful clay sculptures. Then he makes a plaster cast and creates a bronze statue. We hope to return another day to have an art session with him.

Whether you celebrate Christmas or not, thank you for following my writing and social media posts. I am blessed to have your friendship and wish you health, happiness, safety, and easeful living.

Irene in the hot air balloon

Riding through our rose garden entrance

Irene at Temple d'Amon (Médinet Habou)

December 28th

Andy rented a bicycle for the rest of our stay here in Luxor. It is large enough for both of us to ride it, and Ani can sit on the back to get from one place to another. Andy said he actually feels safer riding a bicycle in traffic than walking. My eyes are open to search for a helmet, but we don't have one yet.

Andy writes:

In the last several years, I have rented/bought bicycles from several places in our travels. Some bicycles were excellent (like the racing bicycle I rented in southern Italy), and some barely worked. In some areas, I need to leave a deposit and show my passport, while in others, they totally trust me and don't ask for any ID. In Hvar, Croatia, I rented a mountain bike (they took a photocopy of my passport and I had to fill out lengthy paperwork). After I had completed everything and handed over my money, they told me I could only ride their full-suspension mountain bike on paved roads. But I hadn't realized that in some countries the brake levers are switched from right to left. In most of the world, the right-hand brake is for the rear wheel, and the left-hand brake is for the front wheel. After riding a bicycle in Japan, I realized something didn't feel right, and I finally realized that the brake levers were reversed. Usually, this isn't a problem for me, as I use both brakes at once, but it could cause an accident if the wrong brake is applied in the wrong situation. I once remember as a kid riding a bike, thinking I only needed the front brake, which didn't end well. Here in Luxor, I rented a Mountain Bicycle (for $2/day), and at first, I was thinking that it was a bit inefficient for a mountain bike to be on paved roads, but then I realized I could just ride right over the speed bumps while the cars/buses/motorcycles had to slow down. Plus, the secondary roads are dirt, and a mountain bike is essential on those roads.

The other day, I was leaving our place, and there was a short but steep gravel/sandy section from our house that led onto the gravel road. I came down this section and saw a man stopped on his motorcycle, talking with someone, so I had to slow down. I put on the right brake as that is my instinct, and the next thing I knew, I had hit the ground hard. As accidents go, this wasn't too bad, but I skinned up my knuckles on my left hand. Of course, it had to be in front of a hookah bar, and I was a bit embarrassed as they all came over to make sure I was ok.

To make matters worse, I wasn't wearing my gloves as I was just going up the road to the bicycle place to rent the bicycle for an additional 50 days. If I were wearing my gloves (as I should have been), it would have been just embarrassing, but no blood. I realized the next day that the bike's brakes had been switched, which is why I wiped out. Now, when I get on this bicycle, I tell myself to use my left hand to brake first, keeping it on the brake to help me remember. My new rule is that when I rent a bicycle (somewhere in the world), I check not only that the brakes actually work, but also which brake handle goes to which wheel.

Andy's rental bike

December 29th

This entry discusses the female generative system. If you are uncomfortable reading about it, skip this one.
Today, I listened to The Moth Radio Hour Podcast titled "In a World…" while making a chocolate cake in our Egyptian kitchen. Storyteller Michael Maina recounts his first job after medical school at a hospital in Kenya. There is a woman who is trying to give birth, and an overworked and tired Michael is called in from his home for this emergency. The woman had a placenta previa, which required her to get a C-section to survive the delivery. There is a cultural belief in Kenya about giving birth naturally via the vaginal canal, and the mother of the patient and the patient herself declined the c-section, saying, "Prepare two graves." Michael sits in the hallway, defeated, waiting for his patient and unborn child to die, when the hospital janitor comes and asks him what is wrong. She listens to Michael, and then, having had a c-section herself, she goes into the room and greets all the members of the family, and explains to the patient about her c-section, even lifting her shirt to show her scar, and she changes their mind about the c-section. Michael can do the surgery, safely deliver the baby, and save the patient.

Here in Egypt, I learned that FGM (female genital mutilation) is a common cultural practice. It has been outlawed, yet the cultural belief that it is best prevails over the law. I remember learning about this in Health class in High School (shoutout to Mrs. Olson), but living here in this culture has made me think deeply about this practice and the weight culture carries in people's actions. Egypt is one of the highest countries, with one website citing 87.2% of women aged 15-49 having undergone the surgery. Type 1 or 2 is most common. It usually happens starting at age 9, typically done before puberty starts. Girls will often have this done to them at the beginning of summer so they can heal at home.
The Washington Post wrote a story titled, "Female cutting debate in Gambia takes surprising turn: to women's pleasure."

The article said that while Gambian lawmakers and religious leaders pushed this year to overturn a ban on female genital cutting, they sparked fears globally that this tiny West African nation might be at the forefront of a regression in the region on women's rights. The effort was unsuccessful, and the ban remains in place. But within conservative Gambia, the debate also had an unexpected consequence: A new focus on women's pleasure. It sparks an open discussion about the topic among people. Including the common practice of men marrying a woman who is cut, then having a mistress who isn't, as the sex is better. There are sex toys that are quietly being sold, and men are learning about foreplay.

Worldschooling has opened my eyes to many things. This is one of the hardest for me to understand.

References

A Network for Grateful Living. Grateful Living. Grateful.org, 2025. Accessed 8 Jan. 2026.

Ban Breathnach, Sarah. *Simple Abundance: A Daybook of Comfort and Joy.* Warner Books, 1995.

Brown, Anna, Pam Laricchia, and Erika Ellis. "EU371: Unschooling Stumbling Blocks: Transitional Ages and Seasons." *Exploring Unschooling Podcast*, Living Joyfully, 26 Sept. 2024, livingjoyfully.ca/blog/2024/09/eu371-unschooling-stumbling-blocks-transitional-ages-and-seasons/.

Doucleff, Michaeleen. *Hunt, Gather, Parent: What Ancient Cultures Can Teach Us About the Lost Art of Raising Happy, Helpful Little Humans.* Avid Reader Press, 2021.

Hari, Johann. *Lost Connections: Uncovering the Real Causes of Depression—and the Unexpected Solutions.* Bloomsbury, 2018.

Lasater, Judith Hanson, and Ike Lasater. *What We Say Matters: Practicing Nonviolent Communication.* Rev. ed., Shambhala, 2022.

O'Donnell, Kate, host. "The Greatest Insights into Hormonal Balance and Women's Health." *Everyday Ayurveda with Kate*, episode 10, HealWithKate.org. 24 Sept. 2024, Guest: Dr. Claudia Welch.

Rosenberg, Marshall B. *Nonviolent Communication.* Training presentation hosted by Joe Public, 3 Feb. 2020.

Salzberg, Sharon. *Lovingkindness: The Revolutionary Art of Happiness.* 25th anniversary ed., Shambhala, 2020.

The Social Dilemma. Directed by Jeff Orlowski, Netflix, 2020.

About the Author

Irene Genelin is a writer, worldschooling parent, unicyclist, Ayurveda enthusiast, home chef, and slow traveler who documents her family's everyday life on the road. She began unicycling at age 11 and traveled the world with her husband, Andy, to attend competitions and take part in long-distance unicycling tours. While unicycle touring, she learned to say "excuse me" in many different languages, her favorite being the German "Entschuldigung, bitte." In 2019, they sold their organic fruit farm in Minnesota, where Irene had learned to refinish hardwood floors, keep bees, host wood-fired oven-building workshops, raise animals for meat, and make unusual vegetables taste good by cooking and infusing them with love. Afterward, they began traveling internationally, weaving learning, movement, and community into their daily lives.

Irene's writing grew out of a desire to stay connected while traveling and to share what she was learning about parenting, place, culture, and living with intention. What began as short reflections shared online gradually became a steady writing practice rooted in observation and curiosity. Her work highlights small moments: shared meals, long journeys, chance conversations, and the rhythms of family life across cultures.

She is interested in self-directed learning, worldschooling, mindfulness, and how travel can deepen connections to others and the wider world. This book is her first self-published work.

If you would like to get in touch, here are the best ways to reach Irene:
Email: igenelin@gmail.com
Facebook: facebook.com/igenelin
Instagram: instagram.com/irenegenelin
Substack: slowtravelirene.substack.com
(This is also where you can find her podcast, The Worldschooling Space.)

www.ingramcontent.com/pod-product-compliance
Lightning Source LLC
Chambersburg PA
CBHW041312120726
48005CB00014B/1971

9 798994 509005